STRESS-FREE

small
talk

STRESS-FREE

small
talk

How to Master the Art of Conversation
and Take Control of Your Social Anxiety

Richard S. Gallagher, LMFT

ROCKRIDGE
PRESS

For general information on our other products and services or to obtain technical support, please contact our Customer Care Department within the U.S. at (866) 744-2665, or outside the U.S. at (510) 253-0500.

Rockridge Press publishes its books in a variety of electronic and print formats. Some content that appears in print may not be available in electronic books, and vice versa.

Cover Designer: Antonio Valverde
Interior Designer: Lindsey Dekker
Photo Art Director/Art Manager: Michael Hardgrove
Editor: Emily Angell
Production Editor: Chris Gage
Illustration © Diego Schtutman/Shutterstock.com, p. V.
Interior art used under license from © Shutterstock.com.

ISBN: Print 978-1-64152-895-5 | eBook 978-1-64152-896-2
R0

To Colleen—
my favorite conversation
partner for 46 years
and counting.

CONTENTS

INTRODUCTION

Welcome, and congratulations on taking your first step toward making small talk with other people a stress-free experience.

Casual conversation, or what is often referred to as "small talk," is part of everyday life for the majority of us. Most of us have been talking—and listening—to each other since we were toddlers. For many people, conversations feel as natural as breathing. You speak. They respond. You in turn respond to their response. The words flow naturally and easily, like a properly struck tennis ball lobbed back and forth over a net.

Yet for others, engaging in small talk is a very different experience. It feels more like being placed on a stage, with the glare of a bright spotlight shining down and the audience waiting on every word. The omnipresent fear is that if they utter anything that is not completely correct, everyone will notice!

As a psychotherapist who specializes in treating anxiety disorders such as fears and phobias, I frequently encounter those who suffer from social anxiety disorder (SAD), or the fear of interacting with other people. A survey led by Dr. Ronald Kessler of Harvard has shown that more than 12 percent of people suffer from this fear over the course of a lifetime, and in some cases, it can be debilitating.

For some people, conversations are so painful and humiliating that they avoid them completely. In my therapy practice, I have treated people who could not go to work, attend school, or in one case, even step outside their house for fear of having to speak to someone. People who suffer from this issue are generally highly intelligent and, more often than you might think, reasonably articulate—but understandably, they worry about the social or emotional consequences of what they say to other people.

But then something magical happens when these same people learn the mechanics of how to make small talk. They are able to go back to class. They start dating. They can choose what they want to do without being as worried about whether other people will engage them. And in some cases, they discover that they have learned how to communicate much better than most people.

The foundational reason behind this is that learning to have a conversation is not quite the same as overcoming other types of fears. It is more similar to learning to play a piano: There are basic building blocks that, once understood, make it much easier to improvise. When an individual is taught the mechanics of how to greet people, ask good questions, provide meaningful self-disclosure, and—most important— acknowledge people so that they feel deeply heard, it replaces fear with confidence.

That is ultimately the point of this book: Small talk is a *skill*, just as learning how to bake a cake from a cookbook is a skill. There are clear phases to every conversation and teachable steps you can take to master each of these phases. If you learn and practice them, you will discover that you really can learn to be confident in any conversation.

This book will teach you how to make small talk in a way that you may not have seen before: as a series of reproducible steps that anyone can do. Combined with a strategy of gradual exposure and mindful awareness, based on principles of cognitive-behavioral therapy (CBT), losing the fear of conversation can be much easier than you might think.

Note that ongoing or debilitating social anxiety should be addressed by a medical professional. This book is not a solution for frequent feelings of high stress or anxiety in social situations, nor is it a replacement for a therapist, medication, or medical treatment, and there is no shame in reaching out for help. If you are currently under the care of a professional, consult with them for personalized advice for your situation, and feel free to show them this book to discuss the possibility of integrating its concepts into your treatment plan.

The good news is that social anxiety and other social fears are highly treatable, and developing skills such as learning to make small talk can be an important part of that treatment. In fact, I often tell my own patients that they are lucky because they are learning social skills that many people are never taught. With the right techniques, making small talk does not have to be scary or anxiety provoking, and the strategies in this book can help you approach these conversations feeling calm, confident, and prepared.

"Conversation. What is it? A Mystery!
It's the art of never seeming bored,
of touching everything with interest,
of pleasing with trifles, of being
fascinating with nothing at all."

—Guy de Maupassant, Sur l'Eau (On the Water) *(1888)*

Chapter 1

Small Talk 101

Small talk is an essential part of life. In business, at events, or stand-ing in line at the grocery store, small talk is something we all have to do if we want to interact with the people and the world around us, build a community, expand our network, and advance in our careers.

These casual conversations are the lifeblood of human interaction, yet at the same time, making small talk can be a source of stress for many people. A great deal of this stress springs from a fear of the unknown. What should I say? How will people react to me? What if I freeze up and don't know how to respond? And what if, heaven forbid, I say something wrong?

An important first step in fear reduction is to better understand the fear. So, to better understand the fear associated with small talk, let's first look at what small talk is, why we do it, and how it works.

What Is Small Talk?

The *Oxford Dictionary* defines small talk as "polite conversation about unimportant or uncontroversial matters, especially as engaged in on social occasions." Put another way, its entire purpose is to *build relationships.* This is why conversations about "unimportant" topics can actually be some of the most important kinds of communication we have with people.

Why does small talk happen in the first place? A tremendous amount of science supports the fact that it occurs for a very simple reason: Psychologists call it "social cognition," which is defined as the science of how we perceive other people. Think of it as an instinctive friend-versus-foe reflex. Experts say that people form their first impressions within the first seven seconds of meeting someone. We all react very differently to friends versus foes, and small talk is one of the most important ways that we send signals to other people about who we are.

Think back to when humans were prehistoric cave people. How did they react when they encountered a new person outside of their cave? The answer would have depended on the intentions of the stranger outside of the cave. Were they looking for a companion to hunt and gather food with? Or were they looking to kill the occupants of the cave and steal their possessions? Human survival *and* the ability to build communities and grow as a species both depended on learning to read signals from other people, and to read them quickly.

Do not be misled by the term "small talk." Casual conversation transmits some very important data between people:

- *It tells them how you feel about them.* Are you trying to engage someone you like and want to know better, or are you impatiently going through the motions with someone who annoys you? Your words, along with your nonverbal communication, such as your posture and body language, can speak volumes about your feelings toward someone.
- *It signals whether they are safe with you or not.* If you are on a first date with someone or encounter someone late at night in an elevator, the first things you say often telegraph your intentions toward them. A mugger, for example, is not likely to start a conversation by talking about what a nice night it is. Likewise, inappropriate sexual comments to a stranger would strongly raise their threat awareness.
- *It tells them whether you share similar personalities or not.* Some people are very practical and like to get right down to business. Others are very empathic and care more about the feelings of the individuals involved. Still others are perfectionists who prefer the world and other people to be a certain way. The casual things you say to another person speak volumes about who you are and whether you both see life the same way.
- *It helps identify where you have common ground.* Relationships are often built on common interests, so when you speak with someone about how the Dodgers are pitching or what kind of vegetables you are planting this year, you help other people discover who you are and what you like—and the same thing is true of how you respond to their interests. Often a shared interest is all you need for opening the door to a lifetime of nourishing conversation and friendship.

- *It turns discussions into relationships.* This is perhaps the most important reason of all for small talk: It builds a human connection with someone, which often goes far beyond the reason for the discussion.

WHERE SMALL TALK MAKES A BIG DIFFERENCE

In recent years, small talk has been the subject of a great deal of behavioral research. The results of this research suggest that small talk has numerous, measurable benefits. Here are just a few:

- Negotiations go much better when they are preceded by small talk (defined as conversations that have nothing to do with the negotiation). For example, Kay-Yut Chen and Marina Krakovsky's book *Secrets of the Moneylab* cites a study led by Nobel Laureate Alvin Roth, where the rate of fair deals rose from 50 to 83 percent by adding some small talk beforehand.
- A 2014 study from the University of British Columbia revealed that the more we have casual relationships with acquaintances—which, by definition, revolve around small talk—the greater a sense of belonging and happiness we feel.
- In a study led by University of Chicago behavioral science researcher Nicholas Epley, commuters in Chicago were asked to either talk to strangers or keep to themselves. The results showed that the group talking with strangers reported significantly more positive commutes that were no less productive.

Why is small talk so uncomfortable for some people? From my experience as a therapist, a big part of it is the misperception of risk. We overestimate how much other people will judge us and underestimate our own ability to connect with them. We learn to see a party as a hostile crowd of people waiting to reject us or a business meeting as an opportunity for failure. In the process we lose sight of our own natural resilience, as well as how much control we have over our conversations.

For example, have you ever been booed by hundreds of people? I have! (Pro tip: Don't tell a story praising the manager of the New York Yankees when you have a speaking engagement in Boston.) But because I could smile, acknowledge my mistake, and get the audience laughing again, things still turned out okay—and several people afterward told me that it was one of the best talks they had ever attended.

The irony is that people who actually do poorly at small talk usually do not care about what they are saying. Conversely, the people who are anxious about it *care too much*. They feel like they are walking on a tightrope, where one small slip will make them fall off for good. They beat themselves up about what they say or how nervous they appear and ruminate about how other people react to them.

Writer Olin Miller once said, "We probably wouldn't worry about what people think of us if we could know how seldom they do." Fatal mistakes in conversation are much rarer than we think. Much more often, people simply fade into the background for being afraid to make small talk in the first place. Learning how to make easy, casual conversation will help you reveal your true self to others and bring you closer to them.

What Is the Purpose of Small Talk and When Is It Used?

The art of good conversation opens more doors for people than almost any other facet of life. It can be of greater importance than one's education, social status, or even work experience. In some cases, it can be life-changing.

For example, long before I became a psychotherapist, I was a customer service executive for a West Coast startup software company. One of our employees was a young truck driver we had hired to make deliveries for us. Every so often, he would stop by and ask questions about our work—and they were *good* questions. He was truly interested in what we were doing, and beneath his gruff exterior, it was clear that he was very intelligent.

This relationship eventually led to my asking him to take on more responsibilities, such as shipping software releases, and he learned quickly and did well. Soon, as our company grew and went public, there were more opportunities for him. He eventually joined our management team as our manager of software operations. What is the moral of this story? Casual conversations helped lead to a great career that would never have happened by his simply sending us his résumé as a truck driver.

Small talk extends into nearly every aspect of our lives. It is for this reason that it is worth looking at the myriad situations in which small talk may be encountered and how we use it in different social and professional settings. The following are some examples of common life situations in which small talk and informal conversations often serve an integral purpose.

Networking

Networking has one purpose: to connect people. One important aspect of networking is the use of small talk, which helps you build human connections that matter as much as, if not more than, your credentials.

Imagine that you are an interviewer at a job fair for unemployed rocket scientists. Two rocket scientists with identical résumés come over to speak with you. Dr. X is cold and aloof and has little to say. Dr. Y confidently shakes your hand, asks you how your visit has been going, shares some of their personal interests, and has good questions about you and your company. Which rocket scientist would you rather bring in for an interview?

The goal of any networking situation is to *first* build a personal connection with the other person and *then* explore opportunities for further connection. As nationally known social networking expert Phil Gerbyshak put it, "Make friends first, and do business last." It would not be an exaggeration to say the most important networking skill you can develop is to simply delight in the company of other people.

Here are some sample settings for small talk in networking:

- An on-campus recruiting event at your school
- A networking event for owners of local small businesses
- A vendor hospitality suite at a conference for people in your profession

Finally, those with a great deal of networking experience will tell you that most networkers fall neatly into one of two categories: those who establish connections that are personable and desirable and those whose desperation to get hired, noticed, or connected is stamped clearly on their foreheads. Your ability to make good small talk about subjects *other* than what people can do for you has a strong influence on which category you will fall into.

Business

All business ultimately revolves around relationships. For example, did you know that the great American industrialists Henry Ford, Harvey Firestone, and Thomas Edison were all personal friends who frequently went camping together?

There is a popular saying that all business is personal, and it is true from the mailroom to the boardroom. People who like you are much more willing to help you, support you, and even promote or make deals with you. More often than not, these good relationships start with people showing an interest in others by engaging in small talk.

For example, I was once involved in a consulting project for which I was warned that finishing my report would require charts and graphs from someone who was often unpleasant and "too busy" to help. So, I stopped by her desk, greeted her by name, noticed a picture of a sharp-looking young military man on her desk who happened to be her son, and got into a nice conversation with her about his career and her job. The result? Everyone was surprised at how much she cooperated with me on this project. I truly believe that if the others had taken the time to get to know her as a real person, they would have had the same good relationship with her that I had.

Small talk is particularly crucial for people like entrepreneurs, salespeople, and small-business owners because they depend directly on client relationships. Good salespeople, for example, know that it is often more important to ask people about their golf game or their family than about whatever they are trying to sell. Good small talk builds credibility and trust, which in turn make it possible to develop deeper business relationships.

Here are some sample settings for small talk in business:

- Working every day with the same group of people whom you have known for years
- Meeting a new supervisor for the first time
- Collaborating with a coworker on a professional project

Finally, in North America, small talk is an important part of the *culture* of doing business. I will never forget attending an evening barbecue at a professional conference where one foreign visitor kept trying to talk business with everyone with whom he engaged. His attempts at conversation were met with mostly puzzled stares and a general lack of interest because everyone else was there to have a good time! In any workplace, small talk is not just an important social skill but an important career skill, as well.

Special Events

Humans are unique among living creatures in that we come together to celebrate significant events in our lives. These personal events include weddings, birthday parties, and religious or national holidays such as Independence Day and Thanksgiving. For instance, the small town where I live in upstate New York has concerts in the park, an annual Old Home Days festival with a parade, and a community dinner held each Election Day. These and other events present opportunities to connect with people in one's regular network or to meet new people and get to know them for the first time. As a result, small talk is the dominant form of conversation at nearly all of these gatherings.

Other situations may involve playing host to family, friends, visitors, VIPs, or celebrities. In all cases, small talk will likely be the platform upon which establishing or maintaining the relationship is built. For example, you are celebrating a family member's graduation or your son's baseball team wants to meet at your house for lunch. In situations like these, having the right words can help everyone be comfortable and feel welcome.

Here are some examples of settings for small talk at special events:

- Getting to know fellow employees at a company picnic
- Welcoming a visiting exchange student to your community
- Catching up with long-lost relatives at a memorial service

Community

The word "community" refers to much more than the place in which one lives. It also defines the network of people who make up one's life. Small talk is an essential part of these personal and professional relationships, which in turn form a big part of the fabric of life.

These connections include people such as neighbors, affinity groups, boards and service organizations, coaches, and many others. In most cases, these relationships are built on a foundation of common interests and shared life experiences. Often, personal and professional lives can become intertwined. For instance, when rock guitarist Jeff "Skunk" Baxter (of Steely Dan and the Doobie Brothers fame) became friends with a neighbor who was a former Pentagon engineer, it eventually led him to a lucrative second career as a missile defense analyst.

Here are some sample settings for small talk in your community:

- Talking with other parents at a school sporting event
- Meeting informally for dinner every month with a group of fellow professionals in your area of work
- Joining a "network" of new parents in your neighborhood

WHAT'S IN A NAME?

Did you know that small talk wasn't always called that? When it was first studied in 1923 by Polish anthropologist Bronislaw Malinowski, he referred to it as "phatic communication." ("Phatic" is a technical term for communication that serves a social purpose, as opposed to transferring information between people.)

Today, "small talk" is a legitimate term in the lexicon of the English language. Similar terms appear in other languages, as well: The French refer to it as *banalités*; Spanish-speaking people call it *charla*; Russians label it *boltovnya*; and Germans, taking a cue from our language, use the similar term *smalltalk*. There is even a term in Latin for it: *parva Disputatio*. In any language, its use is universal.

Personal Life

For many people, their personal lives revolve around their family, children at home, and/or a significant other. If you are romantically involved or have a partner in your personal life, how did you fall in love? Did you walk up to them and say, "Hi there, I would like to evaluate our mutual interest in a possible romantic relationship?" More likely, you probably noticed something about them and started a conversation about it. If you still have a good relationship, I'll bet that the ratio of small talk to business in your relationship is still very high.

Here are some examples of settings involving the use of small talk in your personal life:

- Sharing a meal with your partner or family
- Going on an outing with your partner or family
- Talking with your partner as you watch a television program or movie together

Exercise: The Benefits of Small Talk

We have just looked at how small talk benefits people in many different situations. Now let's look at how small talk can benefit *you*.

Think about what kinds of things you would love to do if you could better engage in small talk with people. Go to more parties? Meet new people as friends? Be more effective in your workplace? Start a brand-new career or build a network of people in a new city?

Make a list of three to five goals that you have that would benefit from improving your ability to engage in small talk. These can be either personal or professional.

Small Talk Is About Human Connection

Thinking about small talk often feels scary and intimi-dating for people, but you can also learn to think about it in terms of meeting new people, reconnecting with old acquaintances, and broadening your network and community. Talking to other people does not have to be stressful and anxiety-inducing if you have the tools and knowledge to prepare yourself and get yourself in the right mind-set.

Small talk is a skill that anyone can learn. Many people think that a conversation involves making up hundreds of words out of thin air. It feels scary and uncertain, and they worry about not knowing what to say. With proper skills, you can do the following:

- Manage your feelings in a social situation
- Know how to start a good conversation with anyone
- Respond intelligently to anything someone says to you
- Use language that makes people feel good
- Bring the conversation to a smooth end whenever you are ready

Think of small-talk skills in the same way as learning to ride a bicycle. As a child, your first time on a bike probably felt wobbly and unfamiliar: It was scary to be balancing on two wheels, not completely knowing how to keep from falling over. But then your parents probably coached you on what to do—what foot to push off from, how to keep your balance by moving forward, how to safely stop and dismount, and much more. Once someone shows you the techniques, and you practice them, the task becomes a lot easier than you once thought.

Understand that you are far from alone. Many famous media personalities and corporate executives struggled with shyness and had to learn how to speak comfortably in public. The list includes television hosts Johnny Carson and David Letterman, billionaire Richard Branson, and comedian Will Ferrell. These people all eventually overcame their natural shyness through practice and experience. If they could learn to communicate well with the public, so can you.

As you learn and practice skills for making small talk, one concept that will help you is that small talk is always about the other person. It isn't really about how you come across but about how you make the other person feel. As you go through this book, you will discover that you

SOCIAL ANXIETY AND SMALL TALK

Having social anxiety does not always mean that someone is a poor conversationalist or struggles with making small talk.

In my experience as a clinician, I would say that close to two-thirds of my patients with social anxiety find it difficult to make small talk. However, the other one-third have no problem whatsoever with the mechanics of casual conversation. They are affable, articulate, and know exactly what to say to people—they just find it uncomfortable.

The good news is that both kinds of anxiety about conversation are highly treatable. However, some people benefit most from learning new skills, while others do better with gradual exposure to and support for situations they fear.

have a great deal of control over making other people feel good.

If you suffer from shyness or social anxiety, this concept of serving others can be a very useful framework because it not only makes people happy, but it also takes the spotlight off you. As you try specific techniques for connecting with others and see how well they work, you will discover that making people feel good can become addictive, in a very positive way. And knowing you can call on these skills anytime will make these situations feel much more comfortable.

Exercise: Listening to Others

The next time you are out in public, listen to other people having casual conversations. What are they saying? How do they respond to each other? More important, do you notice any common patterns in how they talk to each other? Be a fly on the wall and do not simply listen passively to people. Try to analyze what people are saying and determine if what they are saying to one another follows a common form or establishes a pattern.

Conclusion

Even though we define small talk around "unimportant" conversations, there is nothing small about it. It is part and parcel of the rhythm of our lives and—as people with social anxiety or shyness are painfully aware—it can be very difficult to escape the need for it.

Fortunately, there is a great deal of hope for people who find small talk uncomfortable. I personally have watched the vast majority of my patients recover from these fears—in most cases, well enough to return to school or work, venture into social situations, or even fall in love. And when this happens, it can powerfully change people's lives for the better.

This leads us to an important point that I would like you to keep in mind as you go through the remaining chapters of this book: Anyone can learn to create effective small talk. With enough time, and, more important, enough practice, these skills can become second nature to anyone. You do not need to be smarter, stronger, or braver to make this happen. You just need to follow the strategies in this book and practice them.

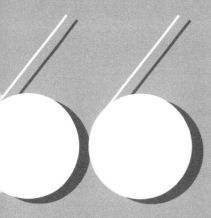

"*I would rather sit on a pumpkin, and have it all to myself, than be crowded on a velvet cushion.*"

—Henry David Thoreau, Walden (1854)

Chapter 2

Navigating Shyness, Introversion, and Anxiety

Before we dive in and explore some strategies for making small talk more comfortable, let's begin by trying to understand our human nature a little better. This chapter will help you learn about shyness, introversion, and anxiety in a social setting, as well as their causes, effects, and why they impact some people more than others.

Having a better understanding of your fears and why you react to certain situations will give you a sense of relief and, more important, can help point you in the right direction to making effective, lasting changes and living a less anxious life. This knowledge will help you realize that if you find conversations with people to be uncomfortable, you are far from alone. Above all, knowing what makes you tick is the first step in having a game plan for being more confident with other people.

Armed with this knowledge, as well as with the skills we discuss later in this book for creating effective dialogue, you can learn to see conversations with people in a new light as a process that you can think through and navigate, one step at a time.

What Is Social Anxiety?

How do you normally feel about interacting with other people? If your answer is "really uncomfortable," the clinical name for that is "social anxiety." *Psychology Today* defines social anxiety disorder (SAD) as "an anxiety disorder characterized by overwhelming anxiety and excessive self-consciousness in everyday social situations."

SAD is the most common anxiety disorder in the world. As we discussed in the introduction, more than 12 percent of people suffer from it over the course of a lifetime. At any given point in time, the percentage of people experiencing social anxiety is about 7 percent. Conservatively, it affects more than 20 million people in the United States alone.

As with any anxiety disorder, SAD is marked by *inappropriate* levels of fear and anxiety in social situations. These can range from low-stakes situations such as casual conversations with people to high-stakes situations such as presentations at work or public speeches. It can be particularly painful and frightening in stressful social situations, such as receiving criticism, encountering confrontation, or being the center of attention. *Psychology Today* notes that this disorder is marked by a "persistent, intense, and chronic fear of being watched and judged by others and of being embarrassed or humiliated by their own actions."

Serious cases of SAD can be disabling, and people whose discomfort with social situations rises to the level of a full-blown fear frequently find that it can also cause emotional and physical symptoms such as depression or insomnia. Moreover, this disorder often limits their ability to function in important areas of their life, including work, school, relationships, or everyday tasks such as shopping and taking care of personal business.

SAD goes far beyond having a simple discomfort with people: It is often a life-altering problem that causes significant distress for sufferers. The good news is that it can be treated in most people. According to the Social Anxiety Association, strategies such as cognitive-behavioral therapy and medication are markedly successful, with a very high success rate backed by research. While SAD treatment is beyond the scope of this book, it is important to realize that there is a great deal of hope for feeling much better in social situations.

Of course, not everyone who struggles with casual conversation and small talk suffers from SAD. Many people find these encounters to be uncomfortable or difficult, even if they do not suffer from extreme anxiety in social situations. Next, we will look at some more common causes for difficult interactions with people, including shyness and introversion.

Shyness, Introversion, and Anxiety

Many people consider the terms "shy," "introverted," and "socially anxious" to mean exactly the same thing. However, nothing could be further from the truth. These terms

Exercise: Mindful Awareness

Does the thought of making small talk—or even reading about it in a book like this—make you feel a little uncomfortable? Try this simple exercise to look at this situation through the lens of mindful awareness:

- First, sit in a comfortable chair and relax.
- Next, picture yourself sitting in this comfortable chair, watching your fears of social interaction play out on a movie screen. Your movie, starring you! Give this movie a name (for example, *Sally's Scary Conversation Fear Strikes Again*).
- Now, turn your attention to the sights, sounds, smells, and tactile feelings of where you are. Remind yourself that you are warm, safe, dry, and—most important—*here*.

What you have just done in this exercise is taken a few minutes out of your life, looked at your anxious thoughts as what they really are (just *thoughts*), and then shifted your attention from these thoughts by grounding yourself in the physical world. This is the core of *mindfulness*, a powerful way to reduce your level of fear over time as you practice shifting your awareness.

overlap, but they have totally different meanings and applications. These differences can be very important in knowing yourself and how you react to social situations.

First, let's look at shyness. Shyness is defined as a sense of discomfort about interacting with people or being in social situations. It is an extremely common trait. According to *Psychology Today*, as many as half the population consider themselves to be shy. It can affect face-to-face encounters with people, remote conversations such as online or telephone chats, or group meetings.

Some shy people may crave the company of others, and others may wish they were alone on a desert island somewhere. Either way, what distinguishes shy people is how uncomfortable it is for them to approach people, respond to them, or hold a conversation with them. Often it is tied in with a fear of looking bad in front of others, and sometimes it can develop in response to having previously endured poor encounters.

Shyness can also be part of deeper issues such as social anxiety, where you are not only uncomfortable with other people but also fear and avoid social encounters. In some ways, the difference between shyness and social anxiety can be seen in terms of the degree of distress that people feel in these situations. Either way, it is a very common shared experience for most people, and a certain amount of it is normal for everyone.

Next, let's consider introversion. In my experience, this is one of the most misunderstood terms in all of psychology. People mistakenly think that an introvert is a shy, withdrawn person who fears social contact. However, introversion has nothing to do with how outgoing you appear. Instead, it is primarily defined by your energy level in social situations.

Introverts may enjoy interacting with people, but these interactions drain a limited supply of energy they have for socializing—and once this energy is used up, they need to get away and recharge. Extroverts, by comparison, gain energy from interacting with others. So, if you go to a party and have a great time but feel drained afterward, you are likely an introvert.

One other defining trait of introverts is that they generally like to have a fully formed thought before they open their mouths to speak, which means they often dislike being "put on the spot" to respond quickly in a social situation. This is a normal part of an introvert's personality. In fact, I often tell introverted patients it is a very good thing that some people like to think before they speak. Extroverts, by comparison, think out loud by talking—and what comes out is not always accurate.

This is one area where knowledge is truly power because, if you are an introvert, you need to know two things about yourself to have effective conversations with people. First, you need to conserve your social energy. Second, because you like to think before talking and not "shoot from the hip," you will do best with prepared questions and responses for common social situations. We will discuss strategies like these and more in the chapters to come.

Finally, how do shyness and introversion relate to anxiety? Sometimes a lot, and sometimes not at all. It completely depends on the person and the situation. It is possible to be shy or introverted and not anxious at all, or it's possible to be very anxious. It's only when this anxiety becomes extreme that we employ a clinical diagnosis such as SAD.

This is why knowing who you are, and how to describe yourself, is an important first step in learning how to have confident conversations with people. One person may be shy because they simply do not know what to say to people, and this can be addressed through learning new skills. Another person may be overwhelmed by anxiety and could benefit from counseling and/or medication. Still another person may need to learn how to react in specific situations. Understanding your own situation will provide valuable data for helping your own social skills and confidence.

FUN FACTS ABOUT INTROVERTS

Introversion is not a "disorder." It is a personality trait that people tend to carry throughout their entire lives that is often measured through common personality tests such as the Myers-Briggs Type Inventory (MBTI). There is nothing wrong with being an introvert, and like most personality traits, it is not something that can or should be changed.

It is important to realize that introverts are not necessarily shy people. In fact, many of them appear outgoing and well-spoken. It is one personality trait that you cannot tell by simply observing another person. Introversion is always about how you feel about socializing with other people, not how you act. For example, many performers, celebrities, politicians, and corporate executives identify as introverts, though they spend a lot of time in the public eye. The list includes Albert Einstein, Steven Spielberg, Al Gore, Michael Jordan, and many others.

ATHLETES WHO OVERCAME SOCIAL ANXIETY

You would think that being able to perform in front of tens of thousands of people every week would mean that someone has mastered being anxious around people—but you would be completely wrong. Here are two examples of athletes who struggled with social anxiety.

Ricky Williams was the top college football player in the nation, winning the Heisman Trophy in 1998. He went on to spend 12 seasons in the NFL, setting rushing records for the Miami Dolphins and becoming only the 26th player in history to run for more than 10,000 yards. But off the field, he found it difficult to do things like go to the store or look people in the eye. Early in his career he was known for reluctantly giving postgame interviews with his helmet still on, his face covered by a dark visor.

Eventually therapy and medication helped Williams gain the ability to socialize more comfortably, and he became an advocate for people suffering from social anxiety. Today he works as a television football analyst and recently starred in the reality television show *Celebrity Big Brother*.

Zack Greinke has been one of the most dominant baseball pitchers of the twenty-first century, winning the American League's Cy Young Award as its top hurler in 2009, with a string of All-Star appearances that continue a decade later. But in 2006 he walked away from the game due to his discomfort interacting with people. In a 2013 interview, he revealed, "It was like having anxiety every day . . . Why am I putting myself through torture when I didn't really want to do it?" Seeking professional treatment helped Greinke return to the mound—and a social life in the clubhouse. According to one of his managers, "He's out here, talking to guys. This is a baseball junkie . . . It's pretty amazing, really."

Differences Between Shyness, Introversion, and Social Anxiety

Shyness, introversion, and social anxiety can each make it difficult to hold a social conversation and engage in small talk, but each has a fundamentally different effect on people:

- Shyness primarily manifests itself as discomfort. It tends to be short-term and situational. Take shy people out of a social situation, and they often feel just fine.
- Introversion is primarily experienced as exhaustion. Social activities drain introverts' limited store of energy, no matter how comfortable they are talking with people.
- SAD primarily shows up as fear. People with SAD don't just find social situations to be uncomfortable—they dread them and are frequently on constant alert to avoid them. In a sense, you could think of social anxiety as shyness on steroids.

Each of these causes for social discomfort can appear to overlap somewhat, particularly when you are surrounded by a group of chatty relatives at a party. But shyness, introversion, and social anxiety are not the same things, and you can easily have one of these issues without the others:

- You can be shy and not be an introvert—for instance, if you enjoy the company of others but find it difficult to make the first contact with them.
- You can be introverted and enjoy socializing, but if you do it for too long, it tires you.

- You can suffer from social anxiety and still be affable and articulate, even if you are very uncomfortable or easily triggered by speaking with other people.

There is one other important distinction between these terms: Only one of them—SAD—represents a clinical diagnosis for a problem. Shyness and introversion are traits that are neither good nor bad, but simply part of the fabric of who you are. People in any of these three categories can potentially benefit from learning better conversation skills and experience a richer and more comfortable social life.

Common Causes

Another difference between shyness, introversion, and social anxiety is that they each have very different causes. Let's examine the common causes of each:

- **Shyness,** when not complicated by excessive anxiety, often has causes of an emotional nature. We react to memories of past social experiences that went poorly, anticipate future bad experiences, worry about other people's reactions, or simply do not know what to say.
- **Introversion** is a personality trait, which is generally viewed as being formed in early childhood through genetics and/or life experience and does not generally change through adolescent and adult life. One 2010 study, for example, showed that personality traits are largely formed by first grade and remain consistent for decades thereafter.
- **SAD,** like other anxiety disorders, is viewed more as a treatable medical and mental health problem.

According to the Mayo Clinic, the three principal causes of SAD are genetics, brain structure, and environmental factors such as parenting or trauma.

In addition to causes such as these, there are common human emotions that spring from our own life experiences when we try to engage other people: fear of judgment, feelings of low self-esteem, feelings of inadequacy, fear of embarrassment, and fear of potential consequences. We'll examine these in the following sections.

YOU CAN'T TELL BY LOOKING

People who don't suffer from SAD themselves often have a mental image of what sufferers are like and how they act— but this image is often completely wrong.

Because social anxiety is a clinical disorder and not a personality type, sufferers vary like any diverse group of humans. In my experience as a clinician, people with social anxiety may be visibly uncomfortable in social situations or may hide their symptoms very well from others. The truth is that any person you meet could potentially suffer from this most common of fears.

In a sense, people who don't "look like" social anxiety sufferers often have it worse, because others may not realize how they feel when people come up to them, start a conversation with them, or invite them to a social event. As a result, these sufferers frequently become skilled at making polite excuses to escape or avoid these situations. Otherwise, they often appear no different from you and me in public.

Fear of Judgment

Nearly every person has memories of being taunted by their peers in school. However, even in adulthood, people may judge us for what we say. Often these fears are exaggerated compared with what people actually think, but the fears are still very real.

Feelings of Low Self-Esteem

Our worst critic often looks back at us from the mirror every morning. Sadly, the negative self-talk we often feed ourselves frequently kicks into overdrive in a social situation.

Feelings of Inadequacy

Many people suffer from what therapists call the "imposter syndrome," in which smart, successful people worry that others will discover they are not as good as they appear. This can then affect our mood and, in turn, our ability to socialize with people.

Fear of Embarrassment

No one wants to look bad in front of other people, and these fears are often magnified when we are in public or social situations. Although actual conversations are usually more forgiving than most of us think, and we can learn to recover from our mistakes, we still worry about what might happen.

Fear of Potential Consequences

The small talk you make with your aunt may be of little consequence, but your small talk with a hiring manager in an interview may determine whether you get hired for an important position. While your strategy for any important conversation should ideally be similar—be prepared and be yourself—the fear of what may happen often looms large.

Beyond common emotions like these, we all have our own personal experiences and feelings that affect our ability to socialize and make small talk. Whatever the cause, never forget that the solution is still the same: learning tools and skills to eventually feel less anxious and master the art of good conversation.

Exercise: Describe Yourself

How would you describe the way you feel about interacting with people? Do any of the definitions of shyness, introversion, or social anxiety we've discussed seem to fit? Make a list of how you would describe your own feelings about engaging people based on what you have read so far.

There is no shame in whatever your feelings about social interactions are. Either way, you have lots of company. These descriptions and your own lived experiences all serve a valuable purpose in helping you learn to understand and manage your reactions.

Do You Ever Feel Like . . . ?

How does it feel to be shy, introverted, or anxious, especially where small talk is concerned? Everyone reacts differently, but there are some common reactions to uncomfortable social situations. Let's examine some of the physical, mental, and emotional symptoms one might experience, as well as the short- and long-term effects on health.

Physical

Physical symptoms associated with being anxious, shy, or introverted include the following:

- Dry mouth
- Shortness of breath
- Increased heart rate
- Dizziness
- Coldness in extremities
- Feeling like legs are turning to jelly
- Extreme sweating
- Blurry vision

All of these are classic symptoms of anxiety, where one feels threatened or trapped, and are associated with the fight-or-flight response, which gives us the focused energy we need to either fight or run away in the face of danger. When something frightens us, adrenaline and cortisol get pumped into our bloodstream, our blood flow is diverted from our extremities to our core, and nonessential bodily functions are shut down. This allows us to be alert, react quickly, and have the strength to flee or defend ourselves.

Symptoms will vary from person to person. In addition, you may also be hypersensitive to how difficult it is to speak in a social situation: Some people report that it feels "hard to push the words out." Anxiety may be emotional in origin, but these physical sensations can often be powerful and frightening.

Mental and Emotional

Mental and emotional symptoms of feeling shy, introverted, or anxious include the following:

- Fear
- Nervousness or excitability
- Panic
- Feeling like you are "jumping out of your skin"
- Shame
- Helplessness and depression
- An urge to escape a situation

Anxiety often exaggerates the way people perceive a situation. For example, a simple social gathering may seem like a pack of wolves ready to attack. Or you may have unrealistic reactions to other people, where you misread their reactions or body language to feel judged or rejected. This can be particularly true when you repeatedly feel you have little control over stressful situations or have been battling anxiety for a long time.

Short- and Long-Term Health Effects

Humans are incredibly resilient creatures, and we are designed to withstand short-term bouts of high levels of anxiety. However, even in the short term, stress can cause health issues such as insomnia, headaches, and gastric problems. According to experts, too much stress over a long period of time can lead to physical issues, including heart problems, high blood pressure, susceptibility to infection, and much more.

Anxiety is an important survival mechanism designed to protect us. It serves us well for occasions such as trying to outrun hungry predators. Today, however, many people feel the same kind of anxiety trying to make small talk with cousins at a family picnic or talking to their boss. This is why learning to manage anxiety and learning conversation skills are both important parts of learning to socialize with people.

Exercise: Slow Down Your Breathing

The mind and body are closely connected, and one tool for reducing anxiety symptoms may be as close as your next breath.

If you are feeling anxious, consciously slow down the rate of your breathing. Relax and let yourself go limp in a chair, exhale deeply, then inhale slowly through your nose to the count of five seconds. (Try counting this off as "one thousand one, one thousand two" and so on.) Hold this breath for a few seconds, then exhale to the count of five seconds. Repeat these steps seven or eight times, then breathe normally.

Understanding Your Triggers

Triggers often differ from one person to the next. Think about what makes *you* anxious in a social situation. Is it a specific type of situation, event, or group of people? What triggers your own anxious thoughts and feelings?

Common triggers include the following:

- The type of person someone is talking to
- The social situation someone is in
- How someone is feeling physically
- How "trapped" someone feels in the setting
- The time of day

The best way to learn and understand your own triggers is to make note of them when (or shortly after) they occur. Writing them down in a journal or on your

WHY TRIGGERS ARE IMPORTANT

Are you triggered by very specific social situations? Knowing triggers like these is the first step in doing what we call cognitive-behavioral therapy, or CBT for short. "Cognitive" means "what you think" and "behavioral" means "what you do." By understanding your triggers, you can start re-examining these scary thoughts and breaking down these situations into small steps that you can learn to re-experience without fear.

We will be covering these ideas in more detail in chapter 3. In the meantime, understand that having specific triggers that you can identify is very good news, and with a little help from CBT, getting well is often much easier than staying fearful.

smartphone may help you see a pattern and, in doing so, help you avoid or confront these triggers in the future.

Exercise: Breaking It Down

When you are in a social situation, having a conversation with someone (or simply trying not to), what does it feel like for you? What is going on physically and emotionally for you in that moment?

Document what these sensations are like for you. Do you get anxious or frightened? Are you aware of physical sensations such as a tight throat, dry mouth, cold extremities, or nausea? Knowing how you normally react is the first step in awareness, as well as tracking your progress over time.

The Benefits of Human Connection

You do have one powerful set of allies when you are learning to socialize with other people—other people.

Connecting with people around us can actually help reduce anxiety and make us feel less alone. Moreover, there is a real reward for learning to master these conversations—the friendship and fellowship of the people we engage. Their presence in our lives can become part of our motivation for getting outside of ourselves and into their world.

The late Dr. Bernardo Carducci, Director of the Shyness Research Institute at Indiana University Southeast, claimed that "the new solution" for shyness is getting involved in the lives of others. He noted that when people learn to focus their attention on others, shyness no longer controls them. In a very real sense, the higher purposes of mastering conversations with others are the benefits of community and connection with other people.

Exercise: Visualize a Goal

Let's try a visualization exercise. Sit in a comfortable chair, close your eyes, and imagine the following:

Think of a person you would like to get closer to or have a better relationship with. Imagine yourself talking confidently with this person and being truly interested in what is happening in their life. Even if you are not ready to have these conversations yet, picture what you would like them to look and feel like.

Imagine this scene in as much detail as possible. Then open your eyes and return to your normal activities.

The Bright Side

While social situations can be scary, there is plenty of reason for hope. Anxiety can be relieved, or at least lessened, by following the advice and techniques that you will read in the chapters that follow. The tools in this book are all proven, evidence-based strategies to assist those with small-talk-related anxiety. There are helpful solutions, tips, and strategies in the pages ahead to help you learn to master good conversations, one small step at a time.

Conclusion

What does anxiety about conversation say about you personally? It says that you are highly intelligent. Anxiety sufferers, as a group, are among the smartest and most talented people I have met. Anxiety is why your ancestors survived in a world of danger and why you have incredible potential.

The good news is that by learning some new strategies, you can harness this intelligence to change the way you look at and react to social situations involving small talk in the future. In the next chapter, we will look at taking the first step toward effective small talk—mastering the mental game of conversation.

"Be not afraid of going slowly,
be afraid only of standing still."

—Chinese proverb

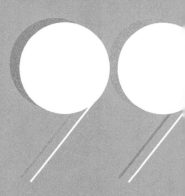

Chapter 3

Step Into Your Fear

This chapter will look at acknowledging and embracing your fears around being in a social situation and doing the necessary preparation so that you can put your best foot forward. This means acknowledging your fears, keeping an open mind to new strategies and advice, and learning how to navigate social situations with more confidence.

One thing that will not occur in this chapter is asking you to make yourself uncomfortable. You have probably already had the experience of "gutting it out" in a difficult social situation or trying awkwardly to make small talk with someone. Those experiences probably did not go well and did not make you feel any better in the long run. "Feel the fear and do it anyway" may be a good motivational slogan, but clinically I do not feel it is an ideal strategy for fears such as these.

Why is this? Because feeling better in social situations requires learning new skills. In my experience, people with social anxiety get better by becoming *more knowledgeable* rather than by becoming *braver*. If you can learn to understand your feelings, have appropriate expectations, and take simple, practical steps to prepare for encounters, you will learn to see such encounters in a new light: as situations you can confidently master with practice.

Everyone Gets a Little Nervous

Nearly everyone has some anxiety in social situations, especially when expected to meet and talk to new people. Therefore, we are all in the same boat when it comes to socializing and making small talk, even for those who look like a pro at it. In fact, many celebrities and famous people admit to being uncomfortable in social situations, too.

So, if your worries about small talk are no different from some of the most talented people in the world, what does that say about you? It means that you have the same potential as anyone to connect with people and make a good impression. It also underscores the importance of learning strategies for doing this well. In this chapter, we will focus on two of the first steps in this process: developing a new mind-set about engaging other people and preparing ahead of time to make effective small talk and handle challenging social situations.

Exercise: Know Your Stress Points

Some people are fine with one-on-one conversations, but the thought of making small talk in a group puts their stomach in knots. Others would rather be locked in a cage with a hungry tiger than be face-to-face with another individual. Still others fear *any* kind of social contact.

What does your relationship with socializing and small talk look like? I want you to assemble two lists:

- First, make a list of all the things you find stressful about conversations. Is it knowing what to say? The other person's reactions? How to break away gracefully?
- Second, list what you perceive as your strengths where making and engaging in conversation is concerned. For example, are you able to talk comfortably with family members or close friends? Do you have a good sense of humor or a keen insight about other people?

Keep both lists to refer to as you start practicing small talk with people. The list of strengths will remind you of what you already do well and help build your confidence, and the list of stresses will help you choose strategies to reduce these stresses as you practice.

HOW TO "REWRITE" A FEARFUL THOUGHT

Has anyone ever told you to change your attitude about something? That advice probably did not help much. However, there is a clinically proven strategy that *can* change the way you think about a fearful situation, which forms the cornerstone of CBT, first developed by psychiatrist Dr. Aaron T. Beck in the late 1950s.

Among mental health professionals, this technique goes by the lofty title of "cognitive restructuring," but you could think of it as simply rewriting the scary stories you tell yourself. Here's how it works:

Step 1. Make a list of your fearful thoughts.
(Do not just assemble them in your head.)

Step 2. Identify specific errors in thinking. Therapists refer to these as "cognitive distortions," and we all have them. Some broad categories of these include exaggeration, prediction, and expectation.

Exaggeration: We tell ourselves something will be horrible or catastrophic, when in reality it is just unpleasant.

Prediction: We assume that something bad will happen, which actually may or may not happen (and most of the time probably will not).

Expectation: We feel people should act a certain way, but they do not because they have different personalities and see the world differently than we do.

Step 3. Rewrite your statements to be undistorted. Your goal here is not to sugarcoat reality. If you do so, your subconscious mind will not believe it, and as a result, you will not feel any better. Instead, your goals are to create *accurate* and *realistic* statements that remove the distortions and, ideally, to discuss what you will *do* about the situation.

Here are some examples:

- **Scary thought:** "I'm not going to be able to handle going to this party!"
- **New thought:** "I may feel uncomfortable if I go to this party. Here is my game plan for how I will try to handle it."
- **Scary thought:** "I'm going to make a fool of myself in front of all of these people."
- **New thought:** "What I say may or may not connect with other people. If it doesn't, I will make adjustments or move on."
- **Scary thought:** "I wish people wouldn't ask me nosy questions at these events."
- **New thought:** "People sometimes *do* ask questions about me. They are trying to get to know me better, and this is their nature. If they do, here is how I will respond."

Keep an Open Mind

People often have very strong mental images of social situations and small talk, and often these images are not good ones. They see these situations as difficult, scary, and threatening. These perceptions, and the anxiety they cause, are often the single biggest problem people have with engaging others.

It would be great if I could simply snap my fingers and tell you not to think that way. You know as well as I do that doing so is not realistic. Our brains are wired to warn us about possible threats, but we can critically examine these thoughts, be aware of them, and start to challenge some of their assumptions. This process, in turn, will make it easier to take the first steps toward confident interactions with people.

Realize that it is important to keep an open mind and not overthink a social situation before you are in it. Respect any feelings of anxiety you might have about these encounters, but at the same time be open to possibilities of discovering new people, new conversations, and new situations. These benefits are waiting for you on the other side of social conversations, and the risks are smaller and more easily managed in real life than you might think. Let's look at some specific steps for changing the way you look at these situations.

Release Control

Let's look at something that causes a great deal of stress and anxiety when we are around other people: wanting to control the situation.

In reality, complete control is an illusion. It is a goal that no one can ever reach. Part of putting yourself in new situations is accepting the fact that things may not go according to plan but that everything likely will work out in the end.

How do you do this? By visualizing yourself embracing imperfection as something that is perfectly okay. This involves telling yourself things that may be the opposite of what you normally think. Here are a few examples:

- Instead of hoping things will go perfectly, imagine having good conversations that share your real self, whatever you might say.

- Instead of desperately wishing that you do not make a mistake, picture yourself confidently handling whatever mistakes may occur.
- Instead of worrying about who might talk to you or how you might break away from someone, have confidence that you will be able to make good choices in these situations.

In other words, try to replace the need for control with evidence that you will be fine with whatever occurs.

The late self-help author Dr. Wayne Dyer once shared a useful quotation from Hindu teacher Nisargadatta Maharaj about this mind-set: "In my world, nothing ever goes wrong." In other words, everything is an experience we can learn and grow from. This is particularly true in a social setting. Having a good conversation with someone is great. So is discovering that you do not really click with someone. So is learning, even with occasional trial and error, what things people like to hear from you. All of it is good.

This concept is one of the core principles of the "cognitive" portion of CBT: change the way you think about a situation. The goal of CBT is not to sugarcoat reality, but rather to compassionately accept things as they really are. In this case, reality is that we are fallible humans who should connect with whomever we wish, do our best, and not beat ourselves up over the fact that we will never do anything perfectly.

Exercise: Visualize Success

Research has shown that our minds react the same way to imagined experiences as they do to real ones. This is why visualization can be a powerful tool to help prepare you for a social event.

Most people already practice visualization every day of their lives by visualizing negative outcomes. This is more commonly known as worrying! Instead, we will flip the script and visualize a successful experience at your next social event. Try these steps:

- Sit back, close your eyes, and picture yourself at the event.
- Imagine yourself as calm, relaxed, and greeting people warmly with a big smile on your face.
- Think of how it will feel to have people really enjoy speaking with you.

Do not worry about what you are saying to people in this exercise or if it is good enough. Just be you! Try this and see how it makes you feel.

Do Not Strive for Perfection

Much of the anxiety surrounding small talk comes from the fact that you might feel the pressure to be, look, and act perfectly. But ironically, to have truly meaningful conversations, you have to let go of perfection and just be yourself. Not everyone will love meeting you. You will make mistakes along the way, and that is okay! Again, we are all human.

When I first started speaking publicly, I felt I had to do it perfectly *or else*—which substantially increased my anxiety. As years went by, I eventually changed this self-talk to something that made me feel much better. I would say to myself, "I can't possibly speak as often as I do without bombing at least twice a year. So, if today is my day for that, oh well—life will still go on." The same strategy will serve you well before you enter a conversation or a social event. Tell yourself, "I'm human, and it's okay to be human. Whatever happens, I will accept it, and life will go on just fine."

The antidote for perfectionism is to give yourself permission to *be* human. This includes giving yourself the permission to fail occasionally. In an ideal world, we would learn the correct social and conversation skills and speak flawlessly thereafter. In reality, we learn to make small talk in exactly the same way that I learned to use chopsticks: Go in there, make a complete mess, and have fun.

This does not mean that mistakes do not hurt sometimes or that we should not try to avoid them. It just means realizing that our goal is to be good, not to be perfect. As author and psychotherapist Dr. Brené Brown notes in her book *The Gifts of Imperfection*, "Perfectionism is a self-destructive and addictive belief system that fuels this primary thought: If I . . . do everything perfectly, I can avoid or minimize the painful feelings of shame, judgment, and blame." Perfection is not a good thing. It is a false goal that does not help us feel—or speak—better.

You Will Say the "Wrong" Thing on Occasion

Do you worry about saying the wrong thing at a social gathering? Well, we *all* say the wrong thing sometimes, and every one of us has moments where we want to melt into the floor. If you are worried about making a blunder or embarrassing yourself, try to accept that it will happen eventually, but do not let that hold you back from new opportunities or meeting new people.

No matter how experienced we are at conversations, there is no escaping the occasional blunder. For instance, many years ago my sister had a best friend in college who always seemed to be getting in trouble. Decades later I was introduced to him at a banquet, and he had become the CEO of one of Canada's largest corporations. To make small talk with him, I reminded him of all his hijinks in college, and he smiled stiffly and nodded. Later I mentioned this to my sister who then informed me that this CEO was a different person with the same nickname as her friend.

While certainly a mistake on my part, at the end of the day I survived it. The CEO probably does not even remember me or the conversation at this point. Most small talk situations are more survivable than you think. Here are three important reasons why:

- **People tolerate mistakes much more than we think**. Think of it this way: When was the last time you thought badly of someone who made an honest mistake in conversation? I'll bet you never even thought about it afterward. More than likely, when you do not favor people it is because of how they act toward you. For example, they may be arrogant, condescending, or disinterested, or never let you get a word in edgewise. Unlike mistakes, these are all things you have full control over.

- **Conversations are surprisingly resilient**. We often think about conversations as though they were fragile pieces of glass that must be handled carefully and could break at any moment. In reality, they have a tremendous margin for error. Therefore, it might be more useful and accurate to view small talk as being more like a rubber ball that can bounce around, hit the walls once in a while, and still turn out okay.
- **You can recover from mistakes**. People do not always stop to think that once they make a gaffe, they still have a lot of control over what to say and do from there. With a good recovery, a mistake can even prove to be a positive event. The box on page 52 discusses some suggestions on how to gracefully move past small talk slip-ups.

There is a built-in level of "give" in most conversations. Interviewers expect people to be a little nervous. People you meet for the first time realize you do not know them well. Older relatives are aware that there is an age or interest gap between the two of you. So, do not worry too much about how you appear. Be yourself, focus on the other person, and plow forward.

STRATEGIES FOR HOW TO RECOVER IF YOU FEEL LIKE YOU SAID THE WRONG THING

Suppose your fears have become a reality. Something came out of your mouth that you wish you could reel back. Here are some strategies that can help make things better again:

- **Own it.** Let people know that you are human, and do it with a smile, if possible. For example, say, "You know, sometimes I say things out loud before I even think about it."
- **Try appropriate humor.** Acting relaxed and confident after a slip can be a very powerful recovery, and good humor can help with this. For example, say, "I've just used up my quota of mistakes for the day!"
- **Apologize.** If your comments have possibly hurt someone, an apology is the very first thing to say because it should be all about that person. The very best apologies avoid the shopworn catchphrase "I'm sorry" and are sincere and genuine. For example, say, "I feel terrible about what I just said, and I respect you a great deal." (If no one was hurt, do not apologize—it draws attention to yourself and puts you in an inferior light, neither of which makes anyone feel better.)
- **Smile and move on.** Sometimes the best response when you say something wrong is *nothing*—because often the very best thing you can offer your listeners after a gaffe is your confidence.

Finally, there is another important reason that mistakes are okay: People want to get to know humans, not perfect automatons. When you press forward and have authentic, imperfect conversations with people, you are sharing a little bit of your humanity with them. More often than you think, the listener will appreciate that you are a real person and feel more closely connected to you. So, relax, be yourself, and learn to let whatever happens in conversation happen.

Exercise: What Would You Say?

One of the best ways to lose a fear of saying the wrong thing is to prepare for how to recover from it. Pick three or four possible gaffes that you worry about saying and write down what you might say to recover from them. Here are a few examples of gaffes:

- You discover that you have been calling someone the wrong name for an entire conversation.
- You are introduced to a couple by someone who says, "Here, meet Dr. Smith." You warmly greet the husband with "Hello, Dr. Smith!" and then discover that his wife is the doctor.
- You mention that you cannot stand a local celebrity, and then you discover that the other person is close friends with him.

Hint: Start by acknowledging your mistake. Then apologize, if needed. Finally, think of how you might confidently engage the other person. For instance, say, "Wow, I had your name totally wrong all along! I apologize for that. I'm sure it's really annoying to hear someone flub up your own name. By the way, I would love to learn a little more about your new position."

Set Yourself Up for Success

When you are getting ready to attend a social event, *invest time in preparation.* Of all the recommended treatments for stage fright, preparation is at the top of the list. The same holds true for speaking informally at a social event.

Thinking about a social situation beforehand not only will help you feel better, but it also will make you a much more effective communicator. Here are some aspects of the meeting to consider:

- **What kind of event is this?** When a group comes together for a shared purpose, it makes for a great topic of conversation. Prepare for making small talk by looking for common themes, such as how the other people are connected to the subject matter of the meeting or what kinds of experiences they have had with it.
- **Where is the event?** The location of this event can inform the kind of audience that will be there and can also serve as a topic of conversation unto itself.

For example, people may be visiting a city for the first time at an out-of-town conference. Conversely, people who live somewhere are often very proud of their hometown and love to talk about it.

- **Who will be there?** If this is a work-related gathering, will the attendees share common interests? Will they primarily be employees or managers? What kinds of things are they there to learn? Are they possibly presenting their own work? For nonwork gatherings, think about how attendees might break down in terms of age, gender, interests, or other characteristics.
- **What are easy topics to discuss? What are the topics to avoid?** Think ahead about what topics would make for good conversation with this group and see the box on page 56 for some suggestions on what to say or what not to say while engaging in small talk.

Last, never assume things about people. Treat each person as a totally new encounter and ask good questions to learn directly from them.

A GUIDE TO CONVERSATION STARTERS

It is always a good idea to have three to five "conversation starters" planned before heading to an event. These should be based on the type of event, the people who will be there, the location, and other factors. The following are examples of good, bad, and ugly topics.

The Good

- **Common shared business interests.** For example, if you are at a convention of lumberjacks, it is probably appropriate to ask about someone's connection to logging.
- **Their interests.** How is their band going? Or their new boat? Or the Little League team they coach? If you know someone's interests—or can find out—this is a perpetual favorite.
- **Learning about the other person.** Do they come here often? What is their favorite sports team? What is their connection with this gathering? People love to talk about themselves.

The Bad

- **The weather.** B-o-r-i-n-g. When was the last time you were ever interested in a discussion about the weather? Small exceptions to this might be granted if, say, you have both just traveled through three feet of snow to get to the meeting.
- **Relationships.** Have you ever asked someone how their wife is only to discover that she is now his ex? Or asked about their kid to find out that Junior just got arrested again? Relationships are okay for small talk if you know someone very well. Otherwise, a better way to learn about them is to stick with a simple "How have you been lately?"

The Ugly

- **Politics.** More friends have been lost over political differences than just about any other topic, particularly in today's polarized environment. Also, your chances of influencing someone else's political views are somewhere between slim and none.
- **Religion.** Similar logic applies here. Unless you are at a religious meeting or convention—and sometimes even then—you normally should know someone quite well before it is safe to discuss their spiritual beliefs or lack thereof.
- **Any kind of criticism.** There is always the risk that you are criticizing something or someone the other person has a connection with, and it is almost always boorish in small talk. Exceptions can be made for things that are universally disliked, such as traffic jams.

Exercise: Your Favorite Openers

What are some of *your* favorite conversation topics? Think about what you most like to share with another person and make a list of opening lines for at least three subjects that would interest you. Here are a few examples:

- Your work or profession
- Your favorite hobby
- Your favorite sport or professional team
- Places you love to visit

Now, come up with good opening lines for each of the items that you included on your list.

Practice Builds Confidence

No one ever gets better at small talk by avoiding social situations. Very few people are naturally great at small talk; the people who you think are pros at working a room probably have years of experience under their belts. Those who are good at it became that way through experience. They practiced making small talk, formally or informally, until it became second nature to them.

An important addition to this is that people also do not get better at small talk by simply reading a book (including this one). Small talk and conversation skills are developed by *doing*. Therefore, it is important to take the time to learn and practice as you read along. This will ensure that you will acquire maximum benefit from these lessons when applied to your own social situations.

Exercise: Team Up with a Partner

Have you ever noticed that professional athletes often practice with each other before a game?

You can use this same principle to become more confident making small talk. Do you know someone with whom you can talk comfortably, such as a partner or family member? If so, set aside time to practice small talk with that person, choose a topic to talk about, and start building your confidence in slow, safe steps.

If you do not have someone to practice with, look at sample conversations online or on television, and practice how you might respond to them. Either way, the important thing is to practice.

Conclusion

The first steps in making good small talk start long before you ever open your mouth. Understanding the mental game of social encounters, changing the way you look at them, and preparing for them will be of tremendous assistance before you even set foot in a social event. More important, these steps will help build the confidence that will make these encounters go well for both you and the listener.

As with any skill, you will find that confidence builds on itself as you continue to practice your self-talk and preparation. Next, we will turn our attention to the first thing that happens when you engage another person in conversation: making a good first impression.

"What ho!" I said.
"What ho!" said Motty.
"What ho! What ho!"
"What ho! What ho! What ho!"
After that it seemed rather difficult
to go on with the conversation."

—P.G. Wodehouse, My Man Jeeves *(1919)*

Chapter 4

Make a Strong First Impression

Do you worry about how you will come across to other people or what kind of first impression you will leave? I have good news for you: If you can make it through the first few seconds, you are normally going to do just fine.

In this chapter, we will explore some practical strategies for making a strong first impression when you walk into a room for an event, a business meeting, a celebration, or another social encounter. Often, understanding how to make eye contact, stand, deliver a solid handshake, and make the best use of other basic social skills for engaging with other people makes a huge difference in how prepared you feel to enter a new social situation.

These small details will also make a big impact in how other people view you. Do you remember the concept of social cognition that we mentioned in chapter 1? You typically have to manage only the first few seconds of an encounter to make a lasting positive impression on most people. Let's look at the specifics of how you can do this.

The Importance of a First Impression

The word "impression" has its roots in the Latin term *impressio*, meaning something that is pressed in. In fact, one of the word's definitions in the dictionary is "a mark impressed on a surface."

This is a pretty good analogy for what first happens between you and another person. You are, in a sense, leaving a mark on them—an impression that lasts long beyond the initial encounter.

What does this have to do with making small talk? Your first impression, in large part, determines another person's receptivity to talking with you. If you make a good one—which most people have a great deal of control over—small talk becomes much easier and much more forgiving. Do not allow this to intimidate you or cause you anxiety. This is actually a very positive thing. Think of people who didn't make a good impression on you. In all likelihood, they either behaved like boors in some way or their personalities did not click with yours. Moreover, they were probably a small minority of the people you have met or socialized with. This means that your own chances of success are extremely high and will get even better with awareness of how first impressions work.

As we mentioned in chapter 1, you literally only have seconds to make a good first impression on people. This is why much of the difficult work of this first impression happens *physically* as well as verbally. Keeping all this in mind, let's start with the very first thing most people notice: your nonverbal body language.

Body Language

What do people read and assume from your body language?

According to body-language expert Joe Navarro, a great deal is learned from one's nonverbal body language. Navarro made a career of reading the motives of criminals and terrorists for the FBI during the Cold War, and today he uses this same knowledge to help people enrich their own lives. In his bestselling book *What Every BODY Is Saying*, he describes the world as "a vivid, dynamic environment where every human interaction resonates with information." Learning how to recognize, interpret, and make use of this information will give you an advantage in social encounters.

The examples we give within this section will largely presume a traditional stand-up conversation at a social event where both individuals are facing one another. However, many of the same principles apply in other settings, such as sitting together at a bar or being at a meal or banquet together. Either way, your goal is to demonstrate confidence and make the other person feel welcome. Let's look at some specific aspects of body language.

Posture

Your parents probably used to tell you to stop slouching and stand up straight. When it comes to first impressions at a social event, they were right. Your posture forms a very important part of your first impression because it is the first thing that people see—even from far across the room.

Good posture, particularly when you are talking to someone or at a public event, starts with the basics: Stand or sit with a natural erect posture, with your hands at your sides or clasped comfortably in your lap. You do not need to stand stiffly at military attention, but rather the goal is to let your body language exude confidence. Avoid shoving your hands in your pockets, clasping your hands behind your back, or being hunched over; these all make you seem less present with the person in front of you.

Your posture also telegraphs your emotions to the other person, sometimes much more powerfully than what you say. As we discussed earlier, anxiety is part of our natural fight-or-flight instinct when we feel threatened. Here is how anxiety often shows up in your posture:

- You avoid looking directly at the other person.
- You step away from them, instead of leaning toward them.
- Your arms and shoulders tend to be in a closed, defensive posture, as though you were protecting yourself from being hit.

With a real threat, such as the risk of a fight, these are all good defensive strategies. In a casual conversation, however, this physical stance sabotages the purpose of the conversation and makes the other person silently feel rejected and unwelcome. This is why, if you find that people sometimes do not warm up to you easily, the first place to start may be how you *stand* instead of what you *say*.

There is another important aspect to your posture that most people do not stop to think about: leaning in. "Leaning in" is much more than the title of a popular business book—it is also a good strategy for your body language. Moreover, it is a good cue for what you should be doing *emotionally,* as well as physically, in a conversation.

When I teach communications skills workshops, one of my first exercises is to have the class break into pairs and ask each other some questions, such as their dream vacation, favorite meal, and ideal travel partner. Then I observe the class interacting with each other. In the majority of cases, most of the participants are leaning toward each other. It is the universal signal of showing interest in another person.

If you are nervous about a conversation, leaning slightly toward the other person sends a powerful signal to them that will make you both feel better. You can do this no matter how you feel, and instead of sensing anxiety, your partner will feel more listened to. This is why leaning in, and posture in general, is an important aspect of mastering the art of small talk.

Finally, pay attention to how close you stand to another person, and respect their personal space. Some people naturally stand close to each other, while others need more distance. This often has a strong cultural context. I have seen people from different cultures practically chase each other backward around the room, as one person keeps moving closer and the other keeps backing up.

Previously mentioned body-language expert Joe Navarro—who was born and raised in Cuba, where people tend to stand physically closer to one another—has a good technique for managing personal space. He suggests stepping forward toward someone when you first meet them and shake their hand, then taking a step back. If they move toward you, then they are comfortable being closer, but if they remain stationary or step back, they are establishing the personal boundaries they are comfortable with. Then you can respect that space for the remainder of the conversation.

Eye Contact

Your eyes transmit a great deal of information about you to another person. They convey your level of interest, your comfort level, and how engaged you are in the person and the conversation. Knowing this is important because, at some levels, you can control these impressions by being aware of good eye contact.

The basic principle of eye contact is to show connection with someone. That is why we call it eye *contact*. As with most forms of body language, there is a balance. On one hand, constantly looking away from someone telegraphs disinterest or discomfort. On the other hand, staring at someone with a fixed gaze would be disconcerting. Aim for natural, regular periodic glances at the other person's eyes as you are talking and try to follow and match their lead for eye contact.

Beyond that, proper eye contact is also a matter of basic etiquette: Do not look around constantly, peer over the other person's shoulder in search of other people, act distracted, or stare at your phone. Your goal should be a warm, friendly level of eye contact that shows interest in the other person.

THE SCIENCE BEHIND EYE CONTACT

What is the biological reason for making eye contact? According to Christopher Bergland, author of *The Athlete's Way*, research links this to the same survival behavior that helped us hunt moving prey with a spear—or nowadays, do things like lock onto a tennis ball and hit it back over the net.

These behaviors are governed by what is known as the vestibular-ocular reflex (VOR). It works together with the cerebellum, one of the most primitive parts of our brain that helped early hunters and gatherers survive. Our heads are constantly in motion, even in a conversation, and the VOR is the neurological system that keeps our eyes locked on a target during these head movements.

People often react positively to appropriate eye contact because they sense you are using this reflex to "target" them (and apparently have learned over the course of history not to presume you are "hunting" them). This may also explain why people on the autism spectrum sometimes struggle with social encounters, because they find it more neurologically difficult to make eye contact. Bergland notes that this is a skill that gets better with practice and points out that, according to research, "maintaining face-to-face human connections is ultimately the key to our happiness, well-being, and longevity."

Your Hands

Hands are tricky. What do you do with them while you are talking to someone? Leave them hanging by your side? Gesture wildly? Snap your fingers to the music and do the rhumba?

There are two main uses of your hands in a conversation: to show confidence with a relaxed, natural posture or to use them as a communications tool.

In the former case, the best use of your hands is to let them hang naturally at your sides, or adopt the traditional "party pose" with a drink in one hand and the other hanging loosely to one side. Does it feel funny to just leave your hands hanging? Depending on where you are standing, it is also okay to "anchor" yourself against a chair or table with one hand. Either way, relax and let your hands rest comfortably—they aren't going anywhere.

In the second case, hand gestures can punctuate our conversation and show engagement toward the other person. As an Irish American, I sometimes joke that if you tied my hands behind my back, I'd be mute! However, such gestures should be used sparingly. When using your hands to make or amplify a point, be sure to move slowly and calmly and keep your hands close to your body—do not flail or jerk around.

Next, be careful about hand gestures that transmit nervousness to the other person. Do not fidget, touch your face, twirl your hair in your hands, or rub your fingers together. Also, try to avoid putting your hands in your pockets—it is comfortable and familiar but could be interpreted as indifference.

Finally, should you ever touch the other person as you are talking? Some people like to do this, and sometimes the gesture is well received. I personally recommend that you avoid touching people you do not know well, particularly if you are a male talking to a female. I've worked with many people who are triggered by the touch of a stranger, owing to factors such as past trauma or sexual abuse, and I feel it is better to avoid the risk in the first place. Instead, use your hands and body language to make the other person feel welcome, at a respectful distance.

Handshakes

Handshakes have been documented as a gesture between people as far back as the 5th century BCE in ancient Greece and other cultures. Reportedly, its purpose was to show that you were not carrying a weapon, by putting your open hand in contact with another person's.

Nowadays we do not typically need to convince people that we are not going to pull out a weapon on them. Nevertheless, a good, strong handshake forms a key part of our first impression with other people. It welcomes the other person, expresses being open to connecting with them, and provides a brief but important moment of human touch. Moreover, it defines our first impression as one of confidence.

A good handshake is a matter of balance: not crushing the other person's hand, but not being like a limp, dead fish either. It should be short and to the point. Grasp the other person's right hand with your right hand with your thumb on top, pump up and down quickly, and then let go. Ideally you should also smile and make eye contact with the recipient as you shake their hand.

In the United States, firm handshakes between people of either gender are a cultural norm. Be aware, however, that people from other cultures may have different norms. Here are a few examples:

- Russians often only shake hands between the same gender.
- Thai people prefer to bow rather than touch, clasping their hands in a gesture known as *wai*. (The higher the status of the other person, the deeper the *wai* should be.)
- In some religious cultures, women and men who are not related do not touch each other.

Be sensitive to other people and cultures and read a person's body language when you extend your hand. If they do not reciprocate, smile, give a cordial and discreet wave with your right hand, and retract your arm. And, of course, when you travel overseas, familiarize yourself with the norms of the country you are visiting.

Exercise: Practice Your Handshake

Find another person, such as a good friend or
family member, and practice introducing yourself
to them with a good handshake. Here are some
things to look for:

- A good approach, including smiling, making
  eye contact, and extending your right hand
- Using the right grip that is neither too firm
  nor too limp
- Pumping once or twice in a way that does
  not feel too rushed, or too long
- Disengaging and returning to a relaxed posture
  for a conversation

Consider having your partner introduce
themselves to you, as well, to see how this feels to
you as a recipient and give each other feedback.
Keep practicing until this process feels easy and
natural to you.

Smile

Another important part of your first impression is a kind, welcoming smile. If you are going to make small talk with someone, you do not want to be frowning when you meet them.

A useful concept to keep in mind here is the concept of a "game face." This is a term from sports, where athletes put themselves in the mind-set of the game before going out on the field. In a social context, you can think of your "game face" as the happy, confident, smiling face you turn on whenever you enter a social gathering. When you know that it is time to socialize, you can make it a point to have your "game face" on.

You have the ability to control the look on your face in a social gathering, and this "game face" is best practiced beforehand and committed to muscle memory so that you can bring it back on command. In my case, for example, I know that I am smiling well enough when I can feel the corners of my mouth turn up. Others practice in front of a mirror so that they know what a good smile feels like.

Finally, remember that it is okay to be yourself when it comes to smiling. If a bright, 100-watt smile feels forced and unnatural to you, a relaxed and pleasant facial expression that fits you better is perfectly fine. Just be aware of how your face might appear to others and be sensitive to putting the people you are talking with at ease.

SMILING AND CULTURE

In the United States, smiling at someone is seen as a sign of respect. Be aware, however, that this is not universal around the world. According to one researcher, there is a good reason for this.

Polish psychologist Dr. Kuba Krys found that in some countries, too much smiling could be seen as a sign that you lack intelligence or are dishonest. According to Dr. Krys, these countries vary in what he calls "uncertainty avoidance"—in other words, how residents feel about how stable and predictable their social systems are, such as courts and health care.

In countries with low uncertainty avoidance, it does not make as much sense to smile most of the time, so a confident smile may arouse suspicion instead of warmth. As writer Olga Khazan notes, her own upbringing with Russian parents taught her that not smiling does not mean that someone is unhappy.

Therefore, if someone does not reciprocate your smile, don't worry. It may just be the culture they were raised in.

Look Like You Are Listening

We talk throughout this book about the concept of "making small talk," but it would be more accurate to call it "*hosting* small talk." Why? Because its real goal is to make the person you are speaking with feel heard and felt.

This means that being an active listener is a key part of small talk. In fact, you will not be able to keep the conversation going if you are not listening to the other person. However, people sometimes misunderstand what listening really is.

Listening is much more than simply the absence of speaking. To be sure, giving someone the time and space to share their story is a big part of listening. However, true listening is a very interactive process, where you give cues that let the other person know that you are hearing and processing what they are saying.

Experts refer to these verbal and physical cues as "minimal encouragers." They are called "minimal" because you are still letting the other person speak and are not taking the floor away from them. They are also "encouragers" because you are making them feel heard and welcome. Here are some examples of these minimal encouragers:

- Nodding your head
- Responding with your facial expressions
- Saying short phrases like, "um-hmm," "I see," "Absolutely," or "Yes!"
- Asking the person, "Can you tell me more about that?"

As you manage your first impressions with others, be aware that good listening involves giving feedback to the other person and not simply remaining silent on your part.

As we go through the strategies in this chapter, always remember that your main impression on another person will revolve around how you make them *feel*. More than anything, this depends much more on listening than on talking.

A SIMPLE TIP FOR IMPROVING YOUR LISTENING SKILLS

There is an easy way to make people feel you are interested in them.

Psychologists call the technique "mirroring." It involves subtly reflecting another person's behaviors back at them. For example, this may include matching their level of eye contact, tone and volume of voice, and gestures.

Good mirroring signals to the other person that you are following their lead and are interested in what they have to say. Not surprisingly, if you do an online search about this technique, many articles about it involve one social setting where it can be particularly effective: going on a date with someone.

Like any good technique, you can take mirroring too far. No one likes having their every gesture mimicked in a way that is obvious. *Psychology Today* columnist Dr. Jeff Thompson pointed out that research shows that in some contexts—such as financial transactions—it can create a negative response. However, in most social settings, a little subtle mirroring can make you seem like a very engaged listener.

The Art of Holding a Drink and Eating Passed Appetizers

Picture this: You are standing across from someone, drink in hand, and the host comes by with a tray of delicious food. It is always a juggling act to hold a drink, eat a passed appetizer, and make small talk with someone you just met. How can you navigate this situation?

A good rule of thumb in this situation is to try to leave at least one hand free at all times. Otherwise, you lose the power of using your hands as a tool in conversation (unless you want to spill your drink or fling an onion ring toward someone). Rest your drink or appetizer on a table, if possible, to take turns eating or drinking. If this is not possible, another strategy is to take small portions of appetizers and consume them quickly.

Remember that a standing conversation should never be mistaken for a meal. For more than brief, casual eating and drinking at a social event, make it a point to sit down, eat properly, and devote your full attention to the person you are talking to.

Do Not Overdrink

Speaking of having a drink in your hand, some people look to that drink as a way to soothe their anxious feelings with other people. Drinking alcohol in moderation is a coping mechanism that can take the edge off one's nerves, but in the long term this is not an effective method for managing social anxiety. Alcohol can make anxiety worse over time and can also loosen inhibitions in a negative way. Therefore, if you choose to drink, it is imperative that you pace and manage your consumption of alcohol in a social setting.

The late shyness researcher Dr. Bernardo Carducci determined that 12 percent of shy people turn to "liquid extroversion," where they self-medicate with alcohol in social situations. However, this is a flawed strategy because alcohol interferes with cognitive functioning (in other words, thinking clearly), and this strategy often leads to overconsumption. More important, his research further suggests that drinking did not teach, nor allow for learning, the social skills that are necessary to develop confidence with other people.

How do you navigate social situations with alcohol if you are prone to anxiety?

- Know your tolerance for alcohol and how you are likely to act when you have been drinking.
- Space out your drinks and have food in your stomach.
- Because drinks often flow freely in social settings, be thoughtfully aware of your rate of alcohol consumption.

GROUNDING YOURSELF

One simple way to feel better without consuming alcohol, before or during a social situation, is to practice *grounding*—a mindfulness technique that pulls you out of your thoughts and into your senses. Here is one that comes to us from Captain Tom Bunn, a pilot-turned-therapist who treats fearful flyers at FearOfFlying.com, called the 5-4-3-2-1 technique:

- Sit in a chair and, with your eyes open, loosely focus your attention on a spot in front of you.
- Now silently count off five things you *see* in your peripheral vision. Then count off five things you *hear*. Then count off five things you feel physically, like your feet on the floor or the collar of your shirt.
- Repeat this step with four of each thing, then three, then two, then one.

Congratulations! You have just taken a three-minute vacation from your racing thoughts and helped yourself feel less anxious.

Because the effects of drinking are often delayed from when you drink, be careful not to let your consumption get ahead of your limits.

- Employ friends as "truth-tellers" (and, if needed, designated drivers) to let you know when you have had enough.

Exercise: Natural Self-Soothing

What alternatives to alcohol could you use to help yourself relax in a social setting? Consider options such as the following:

- Deep breathing
- Relaxation exercises
- Talking to a trusted friend
- Meditation
- Visualizing yourself acting calmly and successfully with people
- Taking a break to regroup
- Grounding exercises, such as the 5-4-3-2-1 exercise described on page 78

Research how you might use self-soothing tools like these, then choose one or more new strategies that might work for you.

- Most important, do not let alcohol serve as a substitute for social and communications skills. For most people, learning how to communicate better is the real long-term strategy for reducing anxiety about making small talk.

Start Slow

While we are on the subject of dealing with anxiety, another important point for any social gathering is to go at your own pace. For example, you should not approach a group of new people if it is going to make your anxiety skyrocket. Start small with one person, then two, then work your way up from there.

When I treat people with social anxiety, I stress the concept of good "outs," or strategies to escape a social situation. This allows you to dose-measure how much of a social situation you expose yourself to, making it easier to expand your boundaries. Success is generally experienced by easing your way into these situations and giving yourself a great deal of control.

Fake Confidence

Many people do not feel confident in a social setting. However, sometimes faking confidence can get you through the initial anxiety-provoking moments of a con-versation and lead more naturally into effective small talk. With practice, you can trick yourself into feeling confident.

For example, when I speak to a large audience, I am often very nervous beforehand. So how do I handle this?

GOING SLOW: A GOOD STRATEGY FOR ANY FEAR

Therapists have a term for easy, gradual exposure to fearful situations: "systematic desensitization."

The term is exactly what it sounds like. We expose people to their fears in very small doses, with lots of support. The goals are to be fully present with the sights, sounds, and sensations of where they are and to learn to be comfortable one small step at a time. Done properly, systematic desensitization often is not scary at all.

Slowly exposing yourself to situations—and learning to be fully present with these small steps—is the "behavioral" part of the CBT approach we discussed earlier, which I practice. Approaching fearful situations in small steps, where you feel safe and could escape if you truly needed to, is often the key to staying with these situations long enough to get used to them.

When I arrive at the place where I am speaking, I do not just walk into the room: I *stride* in confidently with a big smile on my face and start shaking hands with people and introducing myself. I joke to myself that if I then pass out on stage from fright, at least I have made a few friends first. This show of confidence helps me feel better and puts my audience at ease.

The same dynamic applies when you are in a social setting. Yes, you may be nervous, but you will be no more nervous with a smile on your face and a confident walking gait, so why not choose a more positive physical presence? It really will help you feel better because it will inform your autonomic nervous system that everything is okay. As a bonus, the way people react to you will rein-force these feelings of confidence.

This skill of acting confident need not just take place when you walk into the room for a social gathering. The night before, the day of, and on that long drive or bus ride to wherever you are going, you can act confident and be present for others, as well. Done well, you will discover that this really does have a positive impact on your actual feelings—and that, with practice, fake confidence is not fake at all.

Exercise: Practicing Confident You

Earlier in this chapter on page 63, you conducted an exercise where you imagined what your ideal first impression would look like. Returning to that, what practical changes would you make, based on what you have read and learned in this chapter?

Write down some of the specific strategies you might try, in areas such as these:

- Posture
- Eye contact
- Handshakes
- Facial expressions
- Handling food and drink
- Your reactions to the other person

Go out and try some of these skills in real life, at a pace that is comfortable for you, and observe how others react to them.

Conclusion

First impressions are not only an important social skill, but they are also often a liberating one for many people. You do not have to learn to speak eloquently for a half hour to create a good social experience. You simply need to take basic steps to make sure that the first few seconds of a social encounter go well. Many people discover that after making a good first impression, they relax, they find themselves liked and accepted, and small talk flows much more easily.

Consider practicing the skills of a first impression in low-stress situations with people you know, and then build from there toward real social situations. The confidence it brings can go a long way toward making these situations much more comfortable. Next, we will look at the heart and soul of small talk: what to say to people.

"The art of conversation is the art of hearing as well as of being heard."

—William Hazlitt, Selected Essays, 1778–1830

Chapter 5

Take Control of the Conversation

We have now reached the heart of making small talk: what to say to another person. This chapter is all about small talk in action. We will explore the mechanics of good conversation, from first introducing yourself to making the conversation count to gracefully taking your leave.

You will learn that proper small talk has a *form* and a *structure*. This is very good news if you normally find it uncomfortable to have casual conversations with people, because good small talk does not mean making up large amounts of dialogue from scratch. It is much more like following a recipe. This chapter will take you through every step of these interactions, from start to finish. First, we will start at the beginning with your introduction.

How to Introduce Yourself

Introductions are an important icebreaker for starting a conversation between two people. A good introduction sets the tone for the dialogue to follow and helps the other person feel comfortable speaking with you. Normally, it has a very simple form:

- First, you say "Hi" or "Hello," followed by introducing yourself ("My name is _____"). If appropriate, extend your hand for a handshake, as discussed in the previous chapter.
- Next, pause and let the other person respond to your greeting. Then acknowledge this person using their name.
- If you feel comfortable doing so, add an appropriate welcoming statement such as "Delighted to meet you" or "Welcome to our house."
- Finally, once you have both introduced yourselves by name, you are welcome to add a brief statement about who you are or why you are there.

Here is an example:

"Hi, I'm Steve."
"Hi, Steve. I'm Gina. I'm part of a local nonprofit agency for cancer survivors."
"It's nice to meet you, Gina. I have tremendous respect for your work. As for me, I'm a lawyer for the local legal aid clinic."

That is all there is to it. In just a few seconds you have met and welcomed someone new and set the tone for a friendly conversation. Here are further suggestions for getting your introduction off on the right foot:

- Practice being positive and enthusiastic for those valuable first few seconds. Remember what you've learned about body language, eye contact, and a good handshake, and speak as confidently as possible.
- Use the other person's name as soon as possible to establish a strong connection.
- Call the other person by the exact name they give you. If they introduce themselves as Robert, they are Robert, not Bob, and if they call themselves Dr. Jones, they are Dr. Jones.

Exercise: Introduce Yourself to Yourself

Assemble a 15-second introduction that includes the following information:

- Your name
- What you do for a living or in the community
- Whatever else you might share with a new person, such as where you are from

Practice this introduction in a mirror—or with a good friend or family member—and rehearse it until it feels comfortable and natural to you. Then, put it in your mental back pocket to be brought out for future use in new social situations.

How to Introduce Someone Else to the Conversation

Another form of introduction that is important to master is how to introduce someone you know to a conversation already in process. This can happen when someone comes over to join you or when you specifically bring them over to meet the people you are speaking with.

In this case, the form is very similar. Use the name of your conversation partner first, then the name of the person you are introducing, and if appropriate, a brief description of the person joining: "John, I'd like you to meet my colleague Dr. Michelle Washington. Dr. Washington is the director of the lab where I work." Then, once again, pause and let both people introduce themselves to each other.

Once the introduction has been made, it is often a nice touch to say something positive about the person joining you: "Dr. Washington and I have been working together for nearly a decade. She's an extremely talented scientist who specializes in working with polymer materials." You can also describe your friendship, or perhaps even use a little gentle humor if appropriate: "Her golf game is *much* better than mine." Then everyone can settle in again for a positive conversation.

How to Enter a Conversation

Two people are chatting at a party. They are engaged in conversation, and their eyes are locked on each other. You would like to join the conversation. Perhaps you know one or both of them, or you would like to get to know them, or perhaps you find what they are talking about interesting. How do you politely join the conversation?

There is a good way and a bad way to do this. You could probably guess the bad way: You hover over them like a fly waiting to land, furtively try to make eye contact with either or both of them, and then abruptly butt in. This is often a very effective approach for making a bad impression.

Now let's look at the good way. There are four key steps to gracefully entering an existing conversation:

1. **Get close, but not too close.** Stand near enough to them so that they can see you and notice your interest in joining in, but not so close that you are invading their space. Then relax, smile, and if one of them catches your eye, give a slight nod. You want to create a physical presence that says you are interested in them but are not desperate to join them if they are engaged with each other.

2. **Read their body language.** Not every conversation *should* be broken into. The people talking may welcome meeting you, or they may be old friends who have not seen each other in 20 years and want to talk privately. Pay attention to how they react silently to your presence. If their body language signals "Hi—we see you and we'll get to you soon," hang out and wait for a good opening. However, if they are physically closed to your presence, this is often a signal that they are focused on each other and do not want to include an outsider right now.

3. **Look for a good opening.** Listen to the conversation and look for one of two signals that you can gracefully break in: One is a pause in the discussion, and the other is when they stop and acknowledge your presence. Do not just jump in verbally, or move closer, in the middle of someone's sentence—wait for the pause or the acknowledgment first. If neither signal comes, it is a sign that they are not open to you right now, in which case you should smile, nod, and move on.

4. **Link to the relationship or the discussion.** Once you have an opening, look for a good "hook" to link you with the conversation:

   - If you know one or both participants, greet them and acknowledge the relationship—for example, "John! Great to see you again! How are you doing?"
   - If you are a stranger, or if the topic at hand is a shared interest, link to the discussion—for example, "I see you're talking about quality management. I really like what you're saying here. This is a big interest of mine too." Good links may include your interest, your expertise, shared connections in the field, or other areas of common ground—and ideally, they should acknowledge or praise the speaker.

Once you have made the "link," introduce yourself to any participants who do not know you, and then join in the conversation. Congratulations! You have now made a good connection.

Universal Topics

Believe it or not, some of the more important tools for small talk may lie in places like your bookshelf, your community, and the media. The more you read, see, and do in the world, the more you will have to say when you meet people. In general, the more you know, the more common ground you can find with strangers.

As you learn things from your usual information sources, start making notes of things that might make good conversation topics. Think of how specific kinds of knowledge might be interesting to people at work, among your interests, and in your social life.

It is also okay to quickly learn about something when an event happens. For example, many years ago I was invited to lecture at a Chinese university. My wife and I taught ourselves some Chinese phrases and learned more about the culture before going. Our hosts were appreciative of our efforts. A small amount of work up front often pays big dividends in connecting with new people.

EASY CONVERSATION TIPS AND TRICKS TO REMEMBER

Here are some additional tips to help conversations go more smoothly:

- Find opportunities to slip in some praise for the person you are speaking with, if possible. Don't gush or be insincere, but even a small number of honest compliments will make *you* seem like a great conversationalist.
- Be yourself and always be friendly, but also consider that talking a little more boldly and firmly will give you authority and credibility.
- If you are feeling anxious about making conversation with someone, slow down, smile, and don't forget to breathe. This will make you appear much less nervous to others.

How Not to Dominate the Conversation

Sometimes when people are nervous about making small talk, they find it difficult to speak. Others, however, respond to anxiety by talking . . . and talking . . . and talking. There is a fine line between confidently participating in small talk and completely dominating the conversation to the point where no one else can get a word in.

Here are some guidelines for giving everyone a fair share of the conversation:

- Scan your partner(s) as you are talking and check in with their body language. Are they waiting to break in and say something? Or are they perhaps losing interest in your story? Let their reactions guide you.
- Pause occasionally and let the other person come up for air. See if they jump in and say something, and if so, gracefully yield the floor to them.
- When someone else finishes speaking, resist the temptation to "top" their stories with yours—appreciate what they are saying and give them the opportunity to bask in their own glory. (However, it is acceptable—and healthy—to share stories that connect with what the other person says.)

Finally, listen to the feedback of people who know you best, such as friends or family members. Do they suggest or politely tell you that you tend to hog the floor? If so, be thoughtfully aware of your conversation in public, and make it a point to let others into the conversation. Remember, this is the art of conversation, not the art of lecturing.

Active Listening: The Key to Keeping a Conversation Going

It is called "small talk," but listening is just as important as, if not more so than, speaking—especially if you are meeting someone for the first time and do not know anything about them.

This leads to a tool that can change everything about your casual conversations: how to acknowledge people so that they really feel listened to. *I firmly believe that this is the most important skill you will learn in this entire book*. If you know how to acknowledge people in a way that makes people feel truly heard and felt, you will stand head and shoulders above most conversationalists, and people will truly enjoy talking with you.

This is the core of a technique known as "active listening" that is often used by therapists, nurses, and other high-contact professions. Here is how it works: Every time someone shares something with you—particularly if it is something personal—choose one of what I call four "octane levels" of acknowledgment, depending on which one feels most appropriate to you. Then plug in the words and respond confidently and compassionately to whatever the other person says.

Here are the four "octane levels" of acknowledgment:

1. **Paraphrasing.** Paraphrasing is simple, mechanical, and easy to use. You simply take what the other person says, rephrase the same thought in your own words, and play it back to the other person. Here are some examples of paraphrasing:

THEM: I just got promoted to vice president at my company.

YOU: Congratulations—that is an impressive promotion.

THEM: My daughter just got in a very scary automobile accident.

YOU: Wow, sounds like she just had a very frightening experience!

THEM: Raising four children feels overwhelming to me sometimes.

YOU: Absolutely, having four kids sounds like a lot of responsibility.

Note that paraphrasing is not parroting or repeating what the other person said. If you were to do that, it would sound insincere. This technique comes to life when you play back the other person's thought with your own words. As with most things in life, this improves with practice.

I consider paraphrasing to be the "bargain basement" of acknowledgment techniques because you are doing nothing more than playing back the other person's thought. But even this basic level of acknowledgment has three powerful benefits: It lets the other person know that you heard them, that you have processed what they are saying, and that it is safe to talk about it. A benefit of this option is that you can pull this technique out of your back pocket and use it anytime.

2. **Observation**. This takes a big step up from paraphrasing. Instead of just playing back the other person's thought, you respond to how they *feel*. Since you cannot

crack someone open and see what they are thinking or feeling, you will need to make your best judgment based on their words, tone of voice, or body language. Do not worry, it is typically okay to guess. Here are some examples of observation:

THEM: I spent all day getting my driver's license renewed.

YOU: That sounds incredibly frustrating!

THEM: My son just graduated from college last week.

YOU: You must be so proud of him.

THEM: I can't stand my office mate.

YOU: I can tell by your tone of voice how frustrated you are about him.

One caution with this technique is that some people are less feeling-oriented than others, and not everyone likes to have their feelings called out publicly, so use your gut. But if you have a good connection with the other person, it can make them feel very much listened to.

3. **Validation**. In this case, you are telling someone that you not only see how they feel, but that those feelings are *valid*—which is why we call it validation. It requires comparing the speaker's feelings to other people's feelings. Here are some examples:

THEM: I've been really anxious about this upcoming dental work.

YOU: I hear you. Just about everyone gets uptight about going to the dentist.

THEM: My boss has been piling a lot of work on me lately.

YOU: That really stinks. No one likes getting dumped on with work.

THEM: Can't wait for Saturday's game!

YOU: Yep. Nothing better than baseball on a summer afternoon.

Validation is not only more powerful than observation (because you are telling people they have a right to feel the way they feel), but it's also safer because you are not calling out their feelings directly. Instead, you are telling them that they are like lots of other people. Therefore, it is a very powerful and effective form of acknowledgment.

4. **Identification**. This most powerful form of acknowledgment puts your own feelings into the equation. This does not necessarily mean that you agree with them—rather, it means you can relate to how they feel. Here are some examples:

THEM: My car repair got delayed by another week, again.

YOU: If that happened to me, I would be furious about it.

THEM: Workplace conflicts like this really bother me.

YOU: You're not alone. I am really sensitive about things like that, too.

THEM: I get really excited about going on vacation somewhere far away.

YOU: Cool, so do I!

Taken together, these four strategies for acknowledgment form the basis for truly active listening. Learn to
do them well, and you will be a master at conversation
with people. As a bonus, if you are shy or introverted,
good acknowledgments serve as a very powerful tool
for assigning the heavy lifting of a discussion back to the
other person. Practice these techniques and you can
confidently respond to *anything* another person might
say to you.

Exercise: Practice the Four Octane Levels

Pick a statement that someone else might say to
you—any statement. Then practice responding
to this statement using each of the four "octane
levels" we just discussed. Here's an example:

Statement: My neighbor's children are driving
me nuts!
Paraphrasing: Sounds like those children are a real
handful.
Observation: That sounds really frustrating!
Validation: No one likes having to deal with a
bunch of annoying kids.
Identification: I hate it when people disturb my
peace and quiet, too.

Ask Questions

Good questions are the fuel of most conversations. They show interest in the person you are speaking with, raise topics of discussion, and help you learn and gather information from them.

Most good questions fall into the same categories that news reporters follow: Who? What? Where? When? How? They can be used as icebreakers to start a conversation, follow up from what the other person is telling you, or switch to a new topic. Here are a few examples:

Icebreaker questions:

"Hi! I see you're a presenter at this conference. What is your talk about?"

"How do you know the host of this party?"

Follow-up questions:

"That is fascinating! How did you manage to do that?"

"How did you feel about that?"

New topic questions:

"I was curious, when is the best time to plant annuals around here?"

"Do you enjoy reading fiction?"

Asking questions of the other person is a great way to keep the conversation going, particularly if you are racking your brain for things to talk about. More important, the right questions can make people feel special and give them a chance to open up about things that are important to them.

When and How to Ask Questions

Of course, too many questions can become too much of a good thing and can turn a friendly conversation into an interrogation. Learning from people and showing interest in them are good, but you do not want to overwhelm your partner with a barrage of questions. Your goal is to tactfully keep a dialogue moving forward with good questions, while letting the other person ask questions of their own.

I teach people a simple rule for when to ask questions: I call it the "three-to-one rule." It means that for every three questions you ask another person, you stop and disclose something about yourself—and perhaps give the other person a chance to ask *you* some questions.

This three-to-one rule is a rough guideline, designed to help shy or introverted people know when to ask questions and when to talk about themselves. You can vary this based on your own personality. Some people may be more comfortable with a five-to-one rule or a two-to-one rule. Follow your gut, read the other person, and do whatever you need to make it an interactive discussion.

Of course, you should also pay attention to what *kinds* of questions to ask. Here are suggested guidelines pertaining to questions:

- Good questions rarely begin with "why" ("Why are you retiring?" "Why did you do that?") because they tend to put people on the spot.
- Avoid questions that are sensitive or inappropriately personal.
- The very best questions speak to people's strengths and joys, so ask about things the other person is proud of or considers important.

In general, questions are a go-to strategy for small talk. It is a good idea to come up with topics for questions ahead of time for a social event. With time and practice, you will have more and better ideas about what works best for you. So, the next time you are wondering what to say to someone, think about what you can *ask*.

HOW TO TALK TO SOMEONE WITH WHOM YOU DISAGREE

It happens sometimes: You end up in a conversation with someone whose views are not aligned with yours. How do you handle these situations?

Many people use an avoidance strategy. They pretend to agree with the other person, say as little as possible, or politely excuse themselves. Others may argue for their own side. (That rarely if ever works.) However, I believe there is an honest and authentic way to engage these people while still being true to who you are.

The key is to use acknowledgment to frame their position as that of a totally reasonable person *first*, and *then* share your view—for example, "You probably believe in X, right? I certainly get that. Your view has some very good points to it. Believe it or not, I actually believe in Y, and here are some of my reasons. . . . But I totally respect your views, as well."

I have had many cordial conversations with people who violently disagree with me by using this technique. If there were a Nobel Prize for communications skills, it would probably go to the person who discovered that you can *acknowledge* someone even when you do not *agree* with them.

Strategies for Conversations That Are Not Going According to Plan

Many people dread small talk because of the fear that the conversation is going to take a turn for the worse, hit a lull, or end up in a very uncomfortable place. In reality, each of these situations can be understood and managed. Here are suggestions for managing them:

- **When a conversation goes sideways**. You say something innocent, and it turns out your partner is passionately against it. Or someone is socially or politically overinvested and starts getting worked up about a topic. What can you do? Far and away, the most important thing here is to acknowledge the other person—no matter how wrong they seem—so that you can bring the conversation in for a smooth emergency landing. When you shame people, even subtly through your body language or lack of response, it often stirs people to go further off the rails. Let them know that you understand where they are coming from, and then make a good excuse and take your leave.

- **A lull in the conversation**. When things go silent, the most important thing to do is *smile* and relax. Learn to be comfortable with longer periods of silence. It is as much the other person's responsibility to keep the conversation going as yours. If things have reached a natural stopping point, the main thing they will remember is your confidence.

- **A bad ending**. Sometimes you will say things that make people unhappy. For example, your beliefs clash with their beliefs, or you disclose a relationship with someone the other person does not like. The solution? Do not try to "fix" the situation. You cannot. Instead, respond as gracefully and respectfully as possible, apologize if you have hurt the other person's feelings, and hope this gracefulness is remembered later when things have calmed down.

QUICK TIPS TO STEER A CONVERSATION

When a conversation seems to be running away from you, here are some quick ways to steer it back toward what *you* want to talk about:

- **Look for linkages**. Find things that connect the other person's conversation to your topic and use those connections to bridge between them—for example, "Yes, that politician is annoying. You know, I'm fascinated by how people speak in public. Here's what I've noticed . . ."
- **Use a framing statement**. Use a statement that announces your intention to change the subject—for example, "That's a good point. By the way, I'd like to switch gears and run something else by you, if that's okay."
- **Take a break**. When you want to keep talking with someone, but not on the current subject, a quick trip to refill your drink or grab an appetizer can often reset the conversation.

How to Politely Exit a Conversation

Most people dread having to leave a conversation, especially if they are not enjoying the other person's company. However, there are strategies you can use to make a tactful exit.

My favorite technique for extricating oneself from a conversation—especially if someone is talking too much—is what I call the "acknowledging close." Here is how it works: Listen to what the other person is saying. Break in and enthusiastically acknowledge the last thing they are saying. Then, while you have the floor, tell them sincerely how nice it has been to speak with them, excuse yourself, and take your leave. Here is an example: "Brian, I could not agree with you more on that point. It has been a pleasure to discuss this with you. I must be getting to my seat before the program begins. Thank you and I hope you have a wonderful evening."

I've personally used this approach many times, and it actually makes most people feel good. Why? Because people expect people who are trying to leave to fidget, squirm, or say as little as possible. Your enthusiasm and acknowledgment will appear very different from that and will make it seem like a graceful departure.

Other tips for a graceful exit include the following:

- A good excuse works wonders, particularly if delivered with a smile. You may need to catch up with someone else, take care of some personal business, or leave for the night. Be sincere but firm, and then take your leave.
- People remember the last thing you say, so make it positive. You do not have to lie and say that it has been

fantastic talking to them, but you can always thank people and hope they have a great evening.

- If all else fails, everyone needs to visit the restroom occasionally!

Exercise: Your Worst-Case Scenario

In real life, bad conversations can be scary. But in the safety of your own imagination, they can be fun! Imagine what a worst-case small-talk conversation might be like for you. Here are a few examples:

- Someone can't stop talking.
- Your partner is very angry about politics and has opposing views from yours.
- The person you are talking to has veered into TMI (too much information) about their life.

Make a list of how you might apply some of the techniques presented within this chapter to make your worst-case conversation go well.

Conclusion

This chapter is much more than a collection of tips on how to make small talk. It is a compilation of strategies that have been proven by behavioral science and through real-life experience. They work! And using them will make you a much stronger and more confident conversationalist.

Remember that good small talk is about technique, and the antidote to anxiety about it revolves around learning and practice. Refer to this chapter often and practice these skills on your own to build your confidence. Next, we will learn how to put the skills of small talk to use in specific situations.

"It's no company at all, when people
know nothing and say nothing."

—*Emily Brontë*, Wuthering Heights *(1847)*

Chapter 6

Special Events

This chapter will concentrate on the specifics of navigating different types of small-talk situations, whether you are attending a networking happy hour, a distant friend's wedding, a business conference, or any other scenario.

Each of these situations requires similar, yet slightly different, tactics. For one thing, your goals for connecting with people may be very different during a business lunch versus a first date. For another, your partners will bring different expectations to different kinds of conversations. Finally, the cultural environment and context of these encounters will have a significant influence on your use of small talk.

Despite the need to acknowledge variances in types of conversations and situations, certain principles are universal to all small talk:

- Greet people warmly.
- Be positive.
- Listen to the other person and acknowledge them.
- Ask good questions and make appropriate self-disclosures.
- Know how to exit the conversation gracefully when it is time.

These are all tools that will help a conversation be more enjoyable, be more productive, and go more smoothly. However, knowing what works best in specific situations will truly make you a master of conversation. Let's break down some of these situations and explore them.

Business

All business is ultimately personal, and the course of business is paved with small talk. Settings for business small talk include interviews, meetings, conferences, business-related social events, and even your day-to-day work life. Some of the things that make business small talk different from other social settings include the following:

- You are speaking as both a person and in a professional role—you are the new intern, the sales representative for your product line, the head of your consulting firm, and so forth.
- Even when you are not talking about your work, you are representing it.

- You are building relationships among people with whom you work or want to work.

With business small talk, you are doing much more than sharing conversation. You are also building a personal "brand" around your competence, interpersonal skills, and knowledge of your profession. People will often keep this personal brand in mind in regard to future opportunities in the field.

Of course, there is much more to business gatherings than business. Often these engagements help develop

SEEING HOW THE OTHER SIDE THINKS

As we discussed in chapter 3, politics is normally not a good topic for small talk, unless you know someone well. But in some professions, it may be inescapable.

An example of this comes from my youngest brother, a successful sales and marketing manager. One day I visited him early in his career and discovered subscriptions to two magazines on his desk: one devoted to a far-right point of view and the other with a completely opposite far-left view.

Perplexed, I asked him about his polar opposite subscriptions, and he subsequently explained that his clients often express strong political opinions to him during the course of conducting business. No matter how they feel, he wanted to have the ability to say, "Yes, I can see exactly where you are coming from." Therefore, he made the decision to stay educated on both sides of every issue. This trait served him very well, as today he is Vice President of Marketing for a successful firm in Silicon Valley.

relationships with friends and colleagues that will last for the rest of your career.

Tactics for Navigating Professional/Business Situations

Whether you are meeting a new colleague at a sales conference, hosting a visitor at your workplace, or getting to know a potential consulting client, there are some common strategies for most casual business conversations. These common strategies include the following:

- **Do your homework**. Business gatherings have one big difference from other social events: People often share their professional expertise. Even if the discussion itself is not completely about business, people will often introduce themselves in terms of what they do. This means that a little knowledge will go a long way in relating to others. The more you can learn ahead of time about the work other people do, the deeper and richer these conversations will be.
- **Be honest.** Of course, be careful not to feign expertise you do not have. Few things land with a greater thud than statements or questions about someone's work that miss the mark or that are completely off-base. It is perfectly okay to be honest about what you do not know and about what you would like to learn about the other person. However, the more you can relate to other people and celebrate their expertise, the better.
- **Understand the culture**. Business events have a culture that is unspoken, but very real. For example, one company or industry may be dynamic and performance-oriented, while others may focus more on people and human service. Whatever it is, this

culture will inform what topics for small talk will be best received by others.

This does not mean that you cannot or should not be your authentic self. Sometimes it may be very appropriate to discuss your son's mental health issues with a sympathetic business colleague or to share your love of football at your nonprofit's enlightenment retreat. We are people first and businesspeople second, and part of good small talk is exposing appropriate parts of ourselves to others. Simply be sensitive to your audience and the context of the gathering.

- **Pay close attention to interviews**. I joke to audiences that hiring managers are trying to find out only two things about you: whether you can do the job and whether you are an axe murderer. (The latter is my tongue-in-cheek metaphor for a bad hire who creates drama and does not work well with other people.) Your résumé and answers to interview questions will help them discover your job skills, but your small talk is just about the only way they can discern how well you socialize with people. With this in mind, be certain to present your best self during even the most casual topics of conversation.

   For example, an interviewer may make small talk with you about how frustrating it is to manage some people. Of course, she is breaking the ice with you. But this is also an opportunity to show her how well you acknowledge her concerns, how you might handle situations like these yourself, and some of the things you notice about managing people. Whether an interviewer is talking with you about their industry or the Dodgers, treat every exchange in terms of what data it might share about you.

Finally, do not try to be perfect. I have interviewed hundreds of people throughout my career, and the ones who raised the most red flags with me were the ones who claimed to handle everything perfectly. This was a red flag to me because I knew that they were lying. Working with other people is never perfect. Remember that you are selling your credibility as much as your credentials, so feel free to share legitimate challenges, frustrations, or mistakes, as long as they are not career-killers.

- **Remember your ABCs**. ABC stands for Always Be Constructive. Business colleagues are very different from personal friends, and a business setting, no matter how informal, is not an appropriate setting for gossip or trash talk. First, even if your partners are smiling and nodding in response, you are branding yourself poorly with negativity. Second, it is a very small world and

Exercise: Who Are You?

Imagine that you have come in for a job interview. After shaking hands, saying hello, and sitting down, the interviewer starts with a simple request: "So, tell me about yourself."

What would you say? Think about how you would describe yourself, what kinds of details you might share, and how long you would talk. Then write a 30- to 60-second summary—roughly 100 to 150 words—of how you would respond to this interviewer.

networks are highly interconnected. The person you criticize today may be your new boss next year. Save your real concerns for private discussions with close colleagues and keep your small talk positive.

Networking

Networking events have one important difference compared with other business and social gatherings: They are focused on connecting people with opportunities. This means that your small talk is often tied to the pursuit of something such as a job, a consulting engagement, a business partnership, or a funding source—or perhaps simply to making personal connections with people in some area of your life.

Although networking conversations have an underlying purpose—namely, getting to know people who can help you in some way—casual small talk plays an important role. Engaging in small talk will help people discover who you are as a person. This is of great importance because what they think of you as a person will have a direct influence on the opportunities you gain through the networking experience.

Tactics for Navigating a Networking Situation

Networking events are great relationship-building opportunities because these relationships can lead to more success in life. This also means that the stakes can be much higher when you are making small talk in a networking context. Strategies for ensuring that these situations go well include the following:

- **Brand yourself**. Networking small talk has one key difference from other kinds of small talk: the importance of quickly sharing who you are with the other person. This includes both your skills for the opportunity at hand and a sense of what you will be like to work with.

  I have studiously avoided using the term "elevator speech" in this book because it implies blurting out a quick summary of yourself in 30 seconds or less. Bad or rushed elevator speeches often do people more harm than good—in fact, in her aptly titled book *Kill the Elevator Speech*, networking expert Felicia Slattery notes, "If you can boil down [all] that you are into an exciting few words, that almost trivializes what you do, your background, history, experience, and who you are." However, in spite of this, it is of great benefit to slip in some key points about yourself during the early stages of a networking conversation. These points could include the following:

  - The kinds of opportunities you are seeking
  - What you love to do and are really good at
  - One or two stories that credential your strengths—for example, "When I was at XYZ Company, here's how I managed to turn around the morale of our customer contact team."

  You also want to share what kind of person you are to work, collaborate, or do business with. In doing so, it is important that you *show* rather than *tell* these traits. (Someone who claims, "I'm a hard worker" often is not.) Try to "brand" yourself by being relaxed and confident, showing interest in the interviewer, and letting your stories demonstrate how you handle situations.

- **Your goal is a relationship, not an opportunity**. This point almost sounds like a paradox: You are seeking an opportunity, but you should not focus on it? Correct. This is not really a paradox at all. As we mentioned earlier in the book, networking pros will tell you that they fundamentally meet two kinds of people at their events: those who are visibly desperate for jobs or partnerships, and those who are not.

  Even if you have been laid off or are unemployed and are really hoping for an opportunity, appearing too focused on landing one will hurt rather than help your chances. First, it hurts your credibility because people will wonder if you are desperate for any-thing, rather than a good fit for the job in question. Second, a sad reality of networking events is that they often attract people who have negative reasons for job-seeking, such as being incompetent or being a problem to work with, and you do not want to be seen that way.

  This is where small talk that builds a relationship is critically important. By all means, say things to brand yourself and express appropriate interest in whatever you are looking for, but never forget that the goals of networking are to get to know people, share casual conversation about mutual topics of interest, and delight in each other's company. The ultimate goal is to build relationships that lead to opportunities.

- **Keep it short**. The purpose of a networking event is networking. In other words, people are there to meet many people, so be careful not to monopolize the time of any one contact.

Exercise: The Story That Defines You

Most of us have stories that define our strengths and personalities. Here are a few examples:

- Your attention to detail saved your employer from making a major mistake
- You resolved an interpersonal conflict between coworkers.
- You took initiative on a project and made it very successful.
- You sold twice as much as everyone else last year.

Think about what story might best define you for a networking contact and write down a one-page summary of this story.

A great many people have talked themselves into opportunities and then out of them by going on too long. Be sensitive to the other person's body language, including gestures such as acting distracted or looking at their watch, and keep an eye out for "closing phrases," such as "It's been nice speaking with you." More important, be friendly, professional, and to the point in your networking contacts.

Casual Lunches and Drinks

"Let's get together for lunch." This is often the opening line for a great deal of how we socialize with other people. It is also a line that strikes fear in the heart of many people with social anxiety, because it means carrying on a conversation with someone for an entire meal. Either way, a casual lunch or drinks with a colleague, an acquaintance, or someone you do not know very well requires its own specific small-talk tactics.

Meeting someone for lunch or a drink is a time-honored way for people to get closer and more connected with each other. It is also a situation you can learn to master with the right strategy—and small talk is an important part of this process. Let's look at how to handle these situations.

Tactics for Navigating Casual Lunches and Drinks

An informal get-together with someone is an opportunity to do more business together, explore opportunities, share experiences, or simply make someone more of a friend. Casual lunches and drinks with people often deepen your relationships with them if handled well, and good small talk serves a key role in this process. Some tips for managing these meetings include the following:

- **Explore the other person's story**. A casual lunch or trip to the bar normally has a purpose that goes beyond talking about hobbies or sports—you are getting to know the other person more deeply. A good opening for small talk is one that lets the other person share more about who they are. Here are a few examples:

  - "How did you get involved in this industry?"
  - "I would love to learn more about your background."
  - "How long have you been here in Montana?"

In each of these cases, you are handing the other person the microphone and letting them disclose as much or as little about themselves as they wish. More important, it opens a dialogue where you both can share experiences or common interests with each other.

- **Be prepared**. People with social anxiety and shyness often worry that a long meeting over a meal or drinks can "run out of gas," where you come up empty about what to say next and get flustered trying to get back on track.

  The best way to prevent this is to have several topics of conversation in mind ahead of time: perhaps career, interests, the local area, or the other person's feelings about something. (Although, as always, avoid topics like politics, religion, or sensitive personal questions with someone you do not know well.)

  Finally, do not worry about lulls in these conversations. They are completely normal. If you pay attention to what happens during a more relaxed meal out with a close friend or family member, you will notice that the two of you are not constantly talking either. Simply relax, smile, be present in the moment, and wait for either of you to naturally restart the dialogue.

- **Know your limits**. In any meeting where alcohol is involved, know ahead of time how you normally react when drinking and what your limits are. One drink may take the edge off social anxiety or shyness in a social situation, but too many can impair your judgment and send your conversation off the rails. Finally, if you are a teetotaler or prefer not to drink while meeting someone, feel free to order something nonalcoholic.

HANDLING THE PRACTICALITIES OF A MEAL WITH SOMEONE YOU DO NOT KNOW

Eating out with friends is simple. You know each other, conversation flows easily, and it is typically clear who is responsible for ordering, tipping, and other services—and if not, it is usually easy to sort it out. But what if you are having lunch with someone you have never met before?

In general, the person who makes the invitation is the host, and the person invited is the guest. Follow the host's lead on conversation and let them set the tone for the meeting: They may want to make small talk or get right down to business.

Normally, the host should make the first move to pay when the check arrives, although if the meeting was mutually beneficial, the guest is welcome to offer. Ultimately, let the host decide. There are exceptions to this: For example, if a prospective client invites a salesperson to lunch, the salesperson still normally pays. Conversely, the guest normally gets first call at ordering the meal. In general, the goal is to know your role and follow it.

Special Events

One unique quality of humans is that we celebrate life events. We celebrate birthdays, reunions, weddings, graduations, and retirements, in addition to myriad other special and celebratory events.

Small talk at a special event is often different from that of a professional gathering, but it is no less important.

Why is that? Because these get-togethers are where we build and grow the human relationships that fuel our lives. Often, they involve people we have not seen in a long time, such as distant family members or old friends. Sharing casual conversation with these people is how we reaffirm these relationships over the course of our lifetimes.

Tactics for Navigating a Special Event

Special events and celebrations are often—but not always—less formal than other kinds of social gatherings. However, a less formal occasion does not mean there are no rules for small talk. What you say to your friends at a bridal shower often matters as much as, if not more than, what you say to your boss at a company meeting. With this in mind, some guidelines for making conversations at these events include the following:

- **Respect the vibe of the event**. We have all seen the person who is too loud and boisterous at a church dinner or the person who tries to make deep and serious conversation in the middle of a joyous family celebration. It is okay to be yourself at a special event, but it is also important to be your *best* self and pay attention to how everyone else is acting.

  I will never forget the first funeral I attended in my large Irish American family as a child. I solemnly went up to the bereaved family members and expressed my deepest sympathies—and they all laughed at me. They were there to have a party! I learned quickly not to walk around with a long face and joined in with everyone. Likewise, any special event will have its own "vibe" depending on the family, culture, or occasion involved. Listen to it, and let it guide the tone and content of your small talk.

- **Get a little more personal**. A family reunion or a block party is not the place to spend all night talking about one's career. It is perfectly fine to catch people up with what is going on in your life—and catch up with what is going on in theirs—but the real substance of personal relationships revolves around common interests and feelings. Whether it is your favorite foods, leisure activities, or how much you cannot stand the traffic in the area anymore—or perhaps something more meaningful, like how you both struggle with raising your children—finding common ground and sharing your personal lives with each other will make for better and more satisfying small talk.

- **Honor the guest of honor**. There is one huge difference between a special event and most social gatherings: Someone invited you to it. As a result, one of your top priorities should be to spend some time with the people who are the hosts or the guests of honor. Going to a special occasion and then ignoring them would be a breach of common courtesy.

  Of course, reality needs to prevail in some situations. If you are at a wedding with 400 guests, you probably cannot (and should not) try to spend a considerable amount of time with the bride and groom. However, you should make it a point to seek your hosts out and thank them, congratulate them, or wish them well—and, if appropriate, get caught up with their lives.

- **Mingle outside of your tribe**. Particularly for family events such as weddings, it is not unusual for people to "clump" for the entire event around the people who are most familiar to them (the bride's family at one table, the groom's family at another, the younger relatives at the other end of the room from the older ones, and so forth).

Hanging out with your own crowd might feel like the most comfortable way to navigate a social event, particularly if you suffer from shyness or social anxiety. If you feel you need to do this, that is perfectly acceptable, but remember that events like these are also a great opportunity for practicing your small-talk skills, including making good introductions, sharing interests, and learning about other people. You will probably be pleasantly surprised at how well most people respond to your overtures, and who you might meet—so if you can, give it a try!

Dating

Going on a date with someone is perhaps one of the highest-stakes areas for small talk. The rewards for doing it well may be as important as falling in love and meeting a life partner.

How important is good conversation on a date? According to the dating site eHarmony.com, it is the most important factor for women, and a close second for men. For nearly a third of daters, their biggest fear is that the conversation will not flow well. Therefore, it would not be an exaggeration to say that small talk is a make-or-break skill for dating.

Ironically, however, this is one area where being shy or introverted may work in your favor. People on first dates are often turned off by traits common to many extroverts, such as talking too much about themselves or being a bore. Dating is one area where your nature—combined with some basic skills—can serve you very well in connecting with people.

Tactics for Navigating Dating

Read any of the many articles about dating, and you will find no lack of advice: Don't be late, don't be creepy, avoid nosy personal questions, and much more. But here, we want to focus on how to have a good conversation on a date. Tips for small talk on a date include the following:

- **Find the right balance**. Most first dates are a tentative dance, where both people share things about themselves and look for the other person's reaction. Keep things light and appropriate at first: Too many compliments, particularly about looks, can be a turn-off. However, noticing something about your date's personality, laugh, or whatever makes them unique can make them feel special. Good acknowledgments—where your date feels heard and accepted—are among the most powerful things you can bring to the conversation.
- **Your goal is to share, not to impress**. The most common dating complaint that I have heard as a family therapist is that someone spent the entire time talking about themselves. Appropriate self-disclosure is absolutely fine, but your goals should be a sense of balance fueled by good questions, a genuine interest in the other person, and sharing authentically who you are.
- **Make it safe for the other person**. This is important for people of both genders, but particularly for women. According to a 2018 survey of over 5,000 women from

the dating site Match.com, the single biggest thing they want on a date is to feel comfortable with the other person. How do you do this? Give the other person a sense of control. Check in with them on things like where they might like to sit, where to go, and what to do, and show them that you respect their boundaries.

- **Discover what your date thinks and feels**. This is, far and away, the most important skill on a date. A 1997 study by a group of psychologists—two of whom, incidentally, married each other—showed that a series of specific personal questions could accelerate falling in love. In my own therapy practice, I frequently use a similar tool—the "Love Maps" quiz developed by compatibility researcher Dr. John Gottman—to help couples learn about each other and grow closer together.

The previously mentioned study led to a widely publicized *New York Times* article in 2015 that listed 36 questions you could ask someone you wanted to fall in love with. These ranged from what a "perfect day" would look like to what you would most regret not having told someone at the end of your life. Some of these questions are frankly a little too personal for a first date, but the principle is still important: Get to know your date as a real person.

HOW TO HANDLE SMALL TALK WHEN FOOD AND DRINKS ARE INVOLVED

Patricia Rossi, NBC daytime correspondent and author of the book *Everyday Etiquette*, coaches celebrities and major league sports teams on how to handle themselves at restaurants, parties, and other settings. She has some useful techniques to share with you on how to keep conversation flowing smoothly when you are out to eat.

Patricia has what she calls the "Three P's." Here are three simple rules to help your get-together flow smoothly:

- **Pausing**. When you first sit down at the table, wait for your host to put their napkin on their lap. Don't start talking—or grabbing things on the table—until the host gets situated first. This gives everyone time to settle in and signals when it's time for casual conversation.
- **Pacing**. Don't eat too fast or too slow. Pace what is happening at the table and go with the flow. This will make you less nervous and help conversation flow more smoothly.
- **Paying**. If you are hosting a group of people, don't let the check show up at the table. Everyone knows that you should be paying—because you invited them. Prevent ending your get-together with an awkward tug-of-war over the bill by discreetly taking care of it in advance when you arrive.

Conclusion

Small talk often has a great deal in common across any situation. For example, you may find yourself talking with someone about their favorite movie or sports team at a sales convention, a dinner party, or a first date. It is the glue that binds human relationships in all walks of life, as well as the basics of friendly, casual conversation that will likely never change.

That said, there are important differences between different kinds of social situations—and more important, different strategies for helping your small talk serve you well in each of them. Mastering these situations is one of the final steps in building your confidence for handling *any* casual conversation with *anyone*. Now, let's close by looking at some specific examples of how to make effective small talk.

"Kind words can be short and easy
to speak, but their echoes are
truly endless."

—Mother Teresa

Chapter 7

Real-Life Scenarios

It is one thing to read about making small talk in a book. It is another to know what to actually say and do in real situations. As with any skill, you will master small talk by putting these skills into practice.

In this final chapter, we will review examples of common small-talk situations that can cause undue stress and anxiety in people, and give advice on how to navigate them like a pro. Think about how these tips might apply to your own situations—and better yet, come up with your own scenarios and think through how you might handle them using the skills in this book. There are ways to confidently master any conversation, and with practice, you will, too.

SITUATION: You enter a party where you do not know anyone except the host.

ADVICE: Being at a large social gathering of strangers is often a social anxiety sufferer's worst nightmare. However, with a few simple steps, you can learn to navigate these situations more comfortably. Here is a strategy that has been successful with many of my patients:

- Start where you are most comfortable: Greet the host and make small talk with them.
- Next, ask them to introduce you to some of the people there. Now you are getting a "warm" introduction, instead of a "cold" one where you have to break the ice.
- Also, ask the host to share some details about the people you will meet—perhaps before the event, in case the host is busy—and use this knowledge to form your opening questions to them. ("I understand you're a pilot for United Airlines. That sounds really cool. Where do you usually fly to?")
- If possible, do some homework ahead of time and have three to five prepared conversation starters ready, as well as three to five things to disclose about yourself so that you can confidently start talking with whomever you meet.
- Do not be afraid to disclose that you sometimes get nervous in social gatherings. People will almost always appreciate your honest feelings, and a surprising number of them will reply, "Me too!"
- Finally, always give yourself an "out" in a situation like this. Pace yourself, find a safe zone on the fringes of the crowd where you can retreat if needed, and

remember that you can break away from people any time you need to. Take small, easy steps to try out your small-talk skills at this party, and gradually expand your comfort zone with practice.

SITUATION: You are flying alone and get seated next to a very chatty passenger.

ADVICE: When people are trapped in a conversation that they do not want to be a party to, they often feel like they have just two lousy options: endure the other person droning on and on or hurt their feelings by asking them to leave them alone.

In reality, there is a third option that works much better: Engage the other person, and then politely set your boundaries. Choose something that represents a good "out" from having a conversation but doesn't blame or shame the other person—for example, having important work to catch up on, a podcast you need to listen to on your headphones, or a presentation to prepare for. Whatever you choose, always make it about you and not them.

The "acknowledging close" technique we discussed in chapter 5 is tailor-made for this situation. Make eye contact with the chatty person. If appropriate, lean toward them with interest. Listen with rapt attention to what they are saying. Give whatever they are saying a heartfelt acknowledgment. Then, when you have the floor, excuse yourself to get back to work and pull out your laptop—or better yet, mention how tired you are, grab one of those insufferably tiny airline pillows, and close your eyes. The other person will feel great, and you will have escaped.

SITUATION: You have to take a client out to lunch by yourself for the first time, and they appear to be very awkward and nervous about making conversation.

ADVICE: You are not the only person on Earth with shyness or social anxiety, and it is not unusual to be in a social situation where you need to make it comfortable for another person, as well as yourself. This person may well be dreading spending an entire meal with someone face-to-face with no escape. Here are some strategies that will serve both of you well:

- Test the waters. Normally, in a longer meeting such as a lunch, the best way to make small talk flow smoothly is to ask open-ended "story" questions. However, a shy person may feel put on the spot with too many questions like these.
- In this case, start with a very simple, nonthreatening question. For example, ask how their work is going, or even how the traffic was getting to the restaurant. Pay close attention to how they respond. If they respond hesitantly or very briefly, they may not relish a very interactive conversation. If this is the case, slow down and take as much of the conversational lead as you can.
- Bring your stories. The three-to-one rule we discussed in chapter 5, where you share something about yourself at least once every three questions, does not really apply when your partner is shy and may not want to be asked too many questions. Focus on sharing things about yourself and let them learn about you as a real, three-dimensional person— and, if possible, try to slip in that you find social

engagements uncomfortable sometimes. (Avoid the use of the word "too" here, unless your partner discloses their discomfort.)

- Create a comfort zone. Talk softly and slowly, use lots of good acknowledgments when your partner does speak, and react to them—silent, talking, or otherwise—in a way that helps them feel welcome exactly the way they are. Be a calm, confident, soothing presence.
- Use purposeful periods of silence. As we discussed in chapter 6, pauses in the conversation are completely normal during a meal out together. (If nothing else, people need to come up for air once in a while and eat!) In this case, sending a signal that you are okay with these pauses will make it much easier on your partner. Take a break when things reach a logical stopping point, smile, and focus on the meal until either of you naturally starts talking again.

Think of how you react in social situations when someone is gentle and accepting with you. Often, treating other shy people this way helps them "come out of their shell" and be more engaged over the course of a lunch meeting.

SITUATION: You are waiting for your colleague at a networking event, but he bails at the last minute.

ADVICE: It can be frustrating to suddenly lose the company of a "support person" at a social event. At the same time, this is an opportunity for networking practice with other people, with the added advantage that you no longer have to be accountable to anyone. You are free to come, go, meet people, and leave as you wish, which can take the pressure off of your own networking.

If you are shy or socially anxious, the first principle here is to take a step toward making small talk that is within your comfort zone. Here are some strategies you might consider:

- Seeking out people who know you or have a connection with your colleague
- Looking for people you have things in common with
- Approaching people who are alone on the fringes of the event so that you do not feel "trapped" in a group (Note that these people may be anxious about networking, too!)

As for what to say, it is always good to have some prepared opening questions based on the event to get people to open up, such as what their experience or expertise is. Since this is a networking event, if possible, practice sharing a short summary of who you are and why you are at the event.

Incidentally, when you do talk to people, a good opening line may be to share—humorously—that you planned to come with a colleague who stood you up at the last minute and you are now trying to do some networking on your own.

SITUATION: You go to a friend's wedding by yourself and get seated at a table with some of their distant relatives.

ADVICE: The best advice in a situation like this is to be pleasant, engage the people around you, and be *you*.

Meeting new people at a social event is an opportunity to get to know them and build new relationships. Politely introduce yourself, ask about their family connections and who they are, and share a little about yourself. And be sure to give credit to the newlyweds, particularly the one your conversation partner is connected with.

Beyond that, since you will probably be at this table for a while, simply be yourself. If you are funny, be funny. If you are reserved, be quiet and confident. Of course, keep your small talk (and your alcohol consumption) appropriate to the event. At a wedding reception, gracefully be prepared to be drowned out by the music and announcements as you celebrate this happy occasion.

As an aside, I was recently in exactly this situation at a large family wedding. I was seated with the other "old people," and the vast majority of them were distant relatives I did not know. The result? We all had a great time, most of them are now my friends on social media, and we all still keep in touch regularly. Therefore, treat situations like these as opportunities, and enjoy the celebration.

SITUATION: You are at a class reunion, you recognize someone who looks familiar, and you greet her warmly with "Hi, Cindy! I haven't seen you in a long time. How are you these days?" She looks up and responds, "My name isn't Cindy."

ADVICE: Mistakes happen to all of us. Naturally, you always have the option of simply saying, "Oops, I'm sorry," and moving on. But this could also be a chance to engage this classmate and get to know her better. Here is how you might do that:

- Own your mistake. Apologize to the other person and, if appropriate, let her know that you wouldn't like being mistaken for another person either.
- Use humor. At a class reunion, it's good to have a prepared line for a situation like this. For example, say, "I used to recognize classmates much better before I got older and started needing three different pairs of glasses!"
- Introduce yourself. Perhaps the best recovery is to let the other person know that, even if she is not Cindy, she is important. Extend your hand, introduce yourself, and ask her name. If she responds positively, make some small talk, such as asking about her or sharing how much you are enjoying the reunion.

Mistakes like these are common, and they are not fatal. Responding with relaxed confidence will help things go well and may even open the opportunity for a new connection with someone.

SITUATION: It is your first week on a new job. You are sitting in the break room eating lunch, and the person at the next table says, "I'm sorry to bother you, but I wish you would chew with your mouth closed. Sounds like that drive me nuts."

ADVICE: People who are shy or socially anxious often dread any kind of criticism or confrontation and do not know how to respond to it.

First, take ownership of the situation by acknowledging that you frustrated them and are happy to fix it. (Note that for some people, this is a legitimate complaint: Many people suffer from *misophonia*, an excruciating clinical sensitivity to other people's chewing and other sounds.)

Next, if you are comfortable, consider showing confidence instead of defensiveness by greeting them. For example, you might say, "My apologies. I can see where that's annoying. I'll be glad to eat more quietly. By the way, my name is George. How are you?"

I personally was in a very similar situation as a teenager, when a coworker complained that I shuffled my feet and it bothered her. I gave a similar response to this, and in my case, it worked out rather well—we have now been married for more than 40 years!

SITUATION: You have just arrived for a job interview. An assistant to the interviewer escorts you into a small room, sits down with you, and then tells you that you both have 5 to 10 minutes to kill before the interviewer arrives. What do you both talk about?

ADVICE: Spending time with someone who is not the interviewer, waiting for the interview to begin, is a common interview situation.

First and foremost, presume that this assistant *is* an interviewer, along with every person you interact with at this organization. Many firms actually do base part of their hiring decisions on how well candidates treat people such as assistants, receptionists, and support staff. It is a good litmus test for how this candidate will work with everyone as part of the company.

Your impression on this assistant will largely revolve around how you make them feel, so here are some dos and don'ts:

- Do express interest in the assistant. Ask about their role in the company, how long they have been there, or anything designed to learn about them, as long as it is not inappropriately personal.
- Do share pleasant small talk, as long as it is positive and professional. Your industry, your city, and their work are all good topics. Conversely, do not assume this assistant shares your interests in hobbies, family, or other personal areas unless they say so.
- Do not sell yourself for the position yet. You will have plenty of opportunities to share your credentials and interest during the interview itself. Right now, the only

thing you are selling is what a polite and confident person you are.

- Do not treat this assistant as a confidante or a source of inside information. For example, do not ask questions like "What's it really like to work here?" However friendly and engaging the assistant is, their allegiance is to their workplace, not to you.
- Finally, avoid sitting in silence without saying anything— this could be perceived as being antisocial or rejecting the assistant. This is one case where small talk forms an important part of your first impression, and the interview itself, so make the most of it.

SITUATION: You are at a family reunion and end up face-to-face with your uncle, who is *extremely* politically opinionated, is a little loud, and has the opposite views as you do. He says hello and starts in immediately with a rant about the state of society. How do you navigate this conversation?

ADVICE: Many families have an uncle like this. The most common response to them is to roll your eyes, endure their rants, or quickly excuse yourself—or worse, challenge them to a battle of wits that you cannot possibly win.

There is a much better strategy, however: good acknowledgment. Remember that *acknowledgment is not the same as agreement*. Here are some phrases you can use as your uncle goes on and on:

- "I can totally see how you feel that way."
- "That sounds incredibly frustrating."
- "You've got a lot of company with those beliefs."
- "That is a very good point."

Your goal here is to paint his position as that of a totally reasonable person—and the more "mustard" you can put on your acknowledgments, the better. Why? Because the more your uncle feels heard and respected, the more likely it is that he will be open to a civil dialogue where you also share your beliefs.

Of course, there are limits to this strategy. If your uncle crosses the line from strong opinions to sexism, racism, homophobia, or other hate speech, you have left the realm of small talk, and you need not acknowledge things that cross your personal boundaries. However, for simple boorishness, this strategy often works wonders for turning it into a cordial, respectful conversation.

SITUATION: You are on a blind date that a friend arranged. You are waiting at a local club to meet this person, who walks in the door. Your eyes lock for the first time. What is the very first thing you say to this person after introducing yourselves?

ADVICE: Many romance novels have begun with the answer to this question. Here, however, we will be a little more pragmatic.

There is no one right answer to this question, but there are some guidelines for what to say and not say. Here are some dos and don'ts for your first impressions on a date:

- Do put the other person at ease. This person has never met you before. They may be eagerly awaiting a great evening with you or worried that you will be a jerk. Starting with kindness and concern is always a good strategy. For example, you might ask where they might be comfortable sitting or offer them a menu.
- Do act glad to see this person. Thank them for getting together with you and let them know that it is nice to meet them.
- Do share a little bit of yourself. Whether it is gentle humor, quiet confidence, or however you see yourself, plan ahead to share something early on that defines who you are.
- Do not get inappropriately personal or too negative. You may be looking for someone to share the depths of your soul with, or you may be having a tough time

at the moment. Neither are great opening topics of conversation.

- Do not bark about the waitstaff, the air-conditioning, the traffic, or anything else. Gentle frustration and good humor are okay—a short fuse is not.
- Do not make inappropriate comments about looks. Telling someone they look warm is fine, but telling them they look hot is a little much for an opening.
- Stay genuine, light, respectful, and kind no matter what.

First impressions are always important, but they are particularly important on a date. Make it a good one—and then relax and be yourself.

SITUATION: You are on a long line to meet one of your favorite celebrities. How do you greet them when you get to the head of the line?

ADVICE: Most public figures try to be kind and gracious with their fans. They are also humans with the same feelings as everyone, which apply to making it through a long, tiring meet-and-greet. Here is how to make it a great encounter:

- Sincere compliments never get old. Did you enjoy the show or their latest album? Let them know. Even if a hundred other people will be saying similar things, they will be glad to hear how much you appreciate their talents. Making people happy is ultimately why performers perform.
- Make it about them, too. Wish them a great tour or performance and thank them for coming to your town.
- Make it short. Get your autograph or selfie, buy a souvenir, and share a quick story if you wish. Then thank them and go. Small talk needs to be really small when there is a long line of people behind you.

Conclusion

You have now learned a great deal about social anxiety, shyness, and the mechanics of making small talk. I sincerely hope that it has been helpful and instructive for you. My wish is for you to see these casual social conversations in a light you may never have seen them in before: as situations anyone can master with the right skills.

This chapter closes the book with a number of real-life situations for small talk, and life will present you with many more. With practice, you will learn—as many of my patients have—that you can handle *any* conversation in *any* situation. In the process, you will discover that these strategies can help you have much *better* conversation skills than most people do. This is my ultimate goal for you: to help you become a confident master of small talk. Good luck!

RESOURCES

The following resources can help you further explore social anxiety, small talk, and the mechanics of good conversation.

Informational Resources on Social Anxiety and Shyness

The Social Anxiety Association (www.socialphobia.org): A nonprofit organization devoted to education and treatment resources for social anxiety.

Psych Central's social anxiety page (https://psychcentral.com /anxiety/social-anxiety-overview/): Information and education resource on social anxiety.

Anxieties.com (www.anxieties.com): An anxiety resource site run by author Dr. Reid Wilson, including an extensive self-help section on social anxiety.

Coaching and Treatment Resources for Social Anxiety

Anxiety and Depression Association of America (www.adaa .org): Provides a nationwide directory of therapists who specialize in treating anxiety disorders such as social anxiety, as well as support groups for social anxiety and other anxiety disorders.

Academy of Cognitive Therapy (www.academyofct.org): A directory of rigorously screened CBT experts experienced in treating anxiety disorders.

Small Talk Coach (www.smalltalkcoach.com): Coaching on small talk and communications skills by this book's author.

Online Support Groups for Social Anxiety

Note that online peer support resources for social anxiety often change over time, so be sure to do a search for current resources. As of this writing, support groups that exist online include the following:

7 Cups (www.7cups.com)

Social Anxiety Support Forum (www.socialanxietysupport.com)

Social Anxiety Support Chat (www.socialanxietysupportchat.com)

Books on Conversation and Communications Skills

Goulston, Mark. *Just Listen: Discover the Secret to Getting Through to Absolutely Anyone*, Revised ed. New York: AMACOM, 2015.

RoAne, Susan. *How to Work a Room, 25th Anniversary Edition: The Ultimate Guide to Making Lasting Connections—In Person and Online*. New York: Avon, 2013.

Rossi, Patricia. *Everyday Etiquette: How to Navigate 101 Common and Uncommon Social Situations*. New York: St. Martin's Griffin, 2011.

Shanley, David. *The Social Anxiety Workbook for Work, Public & Social Life: Strategies to Decrease Shyness and Increase Confidence in Any Situation*. San Antonio, TX: Althea Press, 2018.

Slattery, Felicia J. *Kill the Elevator Speech: Stop Selling, Start Connecting*. Shippensburg, PA: Sound Wisdom, 2014.

REFERENCES

Introduction

Kessler, Ronald, Patricia Berglund, Olga Demler, Robert Jin, Kathleen Merikangas, and Ellen Walters. "Lifetime Prevalence and Age-of-Onset Distributions of DSM-IV Disorders in the National Comorbidity Survey Replication." *Arch Gen Psychiatry* 62, no. 6 (2005): 593–602. https://doi.org/10.1001/archpsyc.62.6.593

Chapter 1

Barker, Eric. "Does Small Talk Make a Big Difference?" *Barking Up the Wrong Tree* (blog). Accessed July 23, 2019. https://www.bakadesuyo.com/2012/02/does-small-talk-make-a-big-difference/.

Bonderud, Doug. "From Music to Missile Defense: The Very Interesting Life of Jeff Baxter." *Northrop Grumman Now.* May 24, 2017. https://now.northropgrumman.com/from-music-to-missile-defense-the-very-interesting-life-of-jeff-baxter/.

Chen, Kay-Yut, and Marina Krakovsky. *Secrets of the Moneylab: How Behavioral Economics Can Improve Your Business.* New York: Portfolio Penguin, 2010.

Cherry, Kendra. "Social Cognition in Psychology." *VeryWellMind.* Last modified August 13, 2019. https://www.verywellmind.com/social-cognition-2795912.

Epley, Nicholas, and Juliana Schroeder. "Mistakenly Seeking Solitude." *Journal of Experimental Psychology: General* 143, no. 5 (2014): 1980–1999. http://dx.doi.org/10.1037/a0037323.

Gerbyshak, Phil. "Phil Gerbyshak—Sales Speaker, Sales Trainer, Social Media Speaker and Strategist." *Phil Gerbyshak*. www .philgerbyshak.com.

The Henry Ford. "The Vagabonds." Accessed July 6, 2019. https: //www.thehenryford.org/collections-and-research/digital-resources /popular-topics/the-vagabonds/.

Nordquist, Richard. "Phatic Communication Definition and Examples." *ThoughtCo*. Last modified March 11, 2019. https://www.thoughtco .com/phatic-communication-1691619.

BrainyQuote. "Olin Miller Quotes." Accessed July 4, 2019. https://www .brainyquote.com/quotes/olin_miller_104682.

Oxford Dictionary, s.v. "small talk," accessed July 4, 2019, https://www.lexico.com/en/definition/small_talk.

Pitts, Anna. "You Only Have 7 Seconds to Make a Strong First Impression." *Business Insider*. April 8, 2013. https://www .businessinsider.com/only-7-seconds-to-make-first-impression -2013-4.

Presentation Training Institute. "Famous People Who Overcame Shyness." June 8, 2018. https://www.presentationtraininginstitute .com/famous-people-who-overcame-shyness/.

Sandstrom, Gillian M. and Elizabeth W. Dunn. "Social Interactions and Well-Being: The Surprising Power of Weak Ties." *Personality and Social Psychology Bulletin*. April 25, 2014. https://doi.org /10.1177/0146167214529799.

Wallace, Jennifer Breheny. "The Benefits of a Little Small Talk." *Wall Street Journal*. September 30, 2016. https://www.wsj.com/articles /the-benefits-of-a-little-small-talk-1475249737.

Chapter 2

American Psychiatric Association. "Social Anxiety Disorder." *Diagnostic and Statistical Manual of Mental Disorders, Fifth Edition (DSM-V)*. Washington, DC: Author, 2013.

Anxiety and Depression Association of America. "Ricky Williams: A Story of Social Anxiety Disorder." Accessed July 30, 2019. https://adaa.org/living-with-anxiety/personal-stories/ricky-williams-story-social-anxiety-disorder.

Carducci, Bernardo. "Shyness: The New Solution." *Psychology Today*. January 1, 2000. https://www.psychologytoday.com/us/articles/200001/shyness-the-new-solution.

Collingwood, Jane. "The Physical Effects of Long-Term Stress." *PsychCentral*. Last modified October 8, 2018. https://psychcentral.com/lib/the-physical-effects-of-long-term-stress/.

ESPN Press Room. "Ricky Williams: College Football Analyst." Accessed July 31, 2019. https://espnpressroom.com/us/bios/ricky-williams/.

Kessler, Ronald C., Wai Tat Chiu, Olga Demler, and Ellen E. Walters. "Prevalence, Severity, and Comorbidity of Twelve-Month DSM-IV Disorders in the National Comorbidity Survey Replication (NCS-R)." *Archives of General Psychiatry* 62, no. 6 (June 2005): 617–627. https://doi.org/10.1001/archpsyc.62.6.617.

Live Science Staff. "Personality Set for Life by 1st Grade, Study Suggests." *Live Science*. August 6, 2010. https://www.livescience.com/8432-personality-set-life-1st-grade-study-suggests.html.

Mayo Clinic. "Social Anxiety Disorder (Social Phobia)." Accessed July 10, 2019. https://www.mayoclinic.org/diseases-conditions/social-anxiety-disorder/symptoms-causes/syc-20353561.

The Myers & Briggs Foundation. "MBTI Basics." Accessed July 9, 2019. https://www.myersbriggs.org/my-mbti-personality-type /mbti-basics/home.htm.

Psychology Today. "Shyness." Accessed July 9, 2019. https://www .psychologytoday.com/us/basics/shyness.

Psychology Today. "Social Anxiety Disorder (Social Phobia)." Accessed July 9, 2019. https://www.psychologytoday.com/us/conditions /social-anxiety-disorder-social-phobia.

Rampton, John. "23 of the Most Amazingly Successful Introverts in History." *Inc Magazine.* July 20, 2015. https://www.inc.com/john -rampton/23-amazingly-successful-introverts-throughout -history.html.

Ross, Dalton. "Anthony Scaramucci Among 12 New Celebrity Big Brother Houseguests." *Entertainment Weekly.* January 13, 2019. https://ew.com/tv/2019/01/13/celebrity-big-brother-cast-anthony -scaramucci/.

Social Anxiety Association. "What Is Social Anxiety Disorder? Symptoms, Treatment, Prevalence, Medications, Insight, Prognosis." Accessed July 9, 2019. https://www.socialphobia.org/social-anxiety -disorder-definition-symptoms-treatment-therapy-medications- insight-prognosis.

Stephen, Eric. "Zack Greinke on Social Anxiety Disorder: 'It Never Really Bothered Me on the Mound.'" *SB Nation—True Blue LA.* February 15, 2013. https://www.truebluela.com/2013/2/15/3992668 /zack-greinke-dodgers-social-anxiety-disorder.

Chapter 3

Brown, Brené. *The Gifts of Imperfection: Let Go of Who You Think You're Supposed to Be and Embrace Who You Are.* Center City, MN: Hazelden, 2010.

Dyer, Wayne W. *Your Sacred Self*. New York: Harper Paperbacks, 1996.

Gallagher, Richard S. *No Bravery Required: A Clinically Proven Program for Fears, Phobias and Social Anxiety*. CreateSpace, 2017.

GoodTherapy. "Cognitive Behavioral Therapy (CBT)." Last modified June 5, 2018. https://www.goodtherapy.org/learn-about-therapy /types/cognitive-behavioral-therapy.

Health Research Foundation. "Famous People with Social Phobia." Accessed July 11, 2019. https://healthresearchfunding.org /famous-people-social-phobia/.

LeVan, Angie. "Seeing Is Believing: The Power of Visualization." *Psychology Today*. December 3, 2009. https: //www.psychologytoday.com/us/blog/flourish/200912/seeing -is-believing-the-power-visualization.

Scott, Elizabeth. "Cognitive Restructuring for Stress Relief." *VeryWellMind*. August 8, 2019. https://www.verywellmind.com /cognitive-restructuring-for-stress-relief-3144919.

WebMD. "Stage Fright (Performance Anxiety)." Accessed July 12, 2019. https://www.webmd.com/anxiety-panic/guide /stage-fright-performance-anxiety.

Chapter 4

Australian Institute of Professional Counsellors. "Encouragers, Paraphrasing and Summarising." *Counselling Connection* (blog). July 21, 2009. https://www.counsellingconnection.com/index .php/2009/07/21/encouragers-paraphrasing-and-summarising/.

Bergland, Christopher. "The Neuroscience of Making Eye Contact." *Psychology Today*. March 25, 2014. https://www.psychologytoday .com/us/blog/the-athletes-way/201403/the-neuroscience -making-eye-contact.

Bunn, Tom, and Lisa Hauptner. "5-4-3-2-1 Exercise" (video). *Soar.* Accessed August 9, 2019. https://www.fearofflying.com/free-video /5-4-3-2-1-exercise.shtml.

Carducci, Bernardo. "Shyness: The New Solution." *Psychology Today.* January 1, 2000. https://www.psychologytoday.com/us /articles/200001/shyness-the-new-solution.

The Free Dictionary, s.v. "systematic desensitization," accessed July 22, 2019, https://www.thefreedictionary.com/systematic+desensitization.

India Today. "Did You Know the Modern Handshake Dates Back to 5th Century BC and It Meant Something Else?" Last modified April 17, 2018. https://www.indiatoday.in/education-today/gk-current-affairs /story/did-you-know-handshake-dates-back-to-5th-century-bc-and -it-had-a-secret-meaning-1213396-2018-04-16.

Khazan, Olga. "Why Some Cultures Frown on Smiling." *The Atlantic.* May 27, 2016. https://www.theatlantic.com/science/archive/2016 /05/culture-and-smiling/483827/.

Krys, Kuba et al. "Be Careful Where You Smile: Culture Shapes Judgments of Intelligence and Honesty of Smiling Individuals." *Journal of Nonverbal Behavior* 40 (2016): 101. https://doi .org/10.1007/s10919-015-0226-4.

Navarro, Joe. "Our Valued Space." *Psychology Today.* February 8, 2012. https://www.psychologytoday.com/us/blog/spycatcher /201202/our-valued-space.

Navarro, Joe, and Marvin Karlins. *What Every BODY Is Saying: An Ex-FBI Agent's Guide to Speed-Reading People.* New York: William Morrow, 2008.

Oxford Dictionary, s.v. "impression," accessed July 13, 2019. https: //www.lexico.com/en/definition/impression.

Thompson, Jeff. "Mimicry and Mirroring Can Be Good . . . or Bad." *Psychology Today*. September 9, 2012. https://www.psychologytoday.com/us/blog/beyond-words/201209/mimicry-and-mirroring-can-be-good-or-bad.

Ward, Alvin. "Proper Handshake Etiquette in 14 Countries." *Mental Floss*. December 28, 2015. http://mentalfloss.com/article/62070/proper-handshake-etiquette-14-countries.

Chapter 5

Gallagher, Richard S. *The Customer Service Survival Kit: What to Say to Defuse Even the Worst Customer Situations*. New York: AMACOM, 2013.

Gallagher, Richard S. *How to Tell Anyone Anything: Breakthrough Techniques for Handling Difficult Conversations at Work*. New York: AMACOM, 2009.

Grohol, John M. "Become a Better Listener: Active Listening." *PsychCentral*. Last modified October 8, 2018. https://psychcentral.com/lib/become-a-better-listener-active-listening/.

Chapter 6

Aron, Arthur et al. "The Experimental Generation of Interpersonal Closeness: A Procedure and Some Preliminary Findings" *Personality and Social Psychology Bulletin* 23, no. 4 (April 1997): 363–377. https://journals.sagepub.com/doi/pdf/10.1177/0146167297234003.

Catron, Mandy Len. "To Fall in Love with Anyone, Do This." *New York Times*. January 9, 2015. http://www.nytimes.com/2015/01/11/fashion/modern-love-to-fall-in-love-with-anyone-do-this.html.

Gottman, John, and Nan Silver. *The Seven Principles for Making Marriage Work: A Practical Guide from the Country's Foremost Relationship Expert*. Revised ed. New York: Harmony, 2015.

Howard, Laken. "What Women Want on a First Date, According to a New Survey." *Bustle*. February 1, 2018. https://www.bustle.com/p/what-women-want-on-a-first-date-according-to-a-new-survey-8073488.

Jones, Daniel. "The 36 Questions That Lead to Love." *New York Times*. January 9, 2015. https://www.nytimes.com/2015/01/11/fashion/no-37-big-wedding-or-small.html.

Mojaverian, Taraneh. "What Do Men and Women Want in a First Date?" *eHarmony Blog*. Accessed July 18, 2019. https://www.eharmony.com/blog/what-do-men-and-women-want-in-a-first-date/#.XTKSgndFyUk.

Rossi, Patricia. *Everyday Etiquette: How to Navigate 101 Common and Uncommon Social Situations*. New York: St. Martin's Griffin, 2011.

Rossi, Patricia. Interview by Richard Gallagher. *Small Talk Etiquette for Social Situations*. Accessed July 22, 2019. https://bit.ly/2yfXTQc.

Slattery, Felicia J. *Kill the Elevator Speech: Stop Selling, Start Connecting*. Shippensburg, PA: Sound Wisdom, 2014.

Chapter 7

Inc.com. "23 Mother Teresa Quotes to Inspire You to Be a Better Person." Accessed October 29, 2019. https://www.inc.com/bill-murphy-jr/23-mother-teresa-quotes-to-inspire-you-to-be-a-slightly-better-person.html

WebMD. "What Is Misophonia?" Accessed July 20, 2019. https://www.webmd.com/mental-health/what-is-misophonia.

INDEX

ACKNOWLEDGMENTS

This book was truly a collaborative effort with the team at Rockridge Press and its parent company Callisto Media, including acquisitions editor Salmon Taymuree, managing editor Emily Angell, lead production manager Kim Ciabattari, and a great many others. It has been an honor and a pleasure to work with all of them.

This project has its roots in an e-book entitled *Conversation 101,* a simple procedural cookbook I developed for the purpose of helping my psychotherapy patients comfortably learn to make small talk. While the book you are holding respects the privacy of their specific cases, as a group they first inspired me to write about this subject many years ago, and I salute their strength and their individual journeys to wellness.

These pages bear the influence of many other people, as well, including my fellow clinicians in the psychotherapy community, other writers and public speakers I am connected with in real life and on social media, and my family and close friends. Three people in particular deserve special mention:

- NBC daytime etiquette correspondent Patricia Rossi, the queen of all things small talk, for being generous of sprit and sharing her time and great advice with this book's readers.
- Los Angeles–based television producer (and my lovely niece) Katie Gallagher for being my millennial and dating correspondent.
- Finally, thanks to Colleen not only for being the love of my life, but also for being a great editor.